1

Meditations for the New Mother

"He shall gather the lambs with his arm, and carry them in his bosom, and shall gently lead those that are with young." ISAIAH 40:11b

Meditations for the New Mother

By

HELEN GOOD BRENNEMAN

Drawings By

ESTHER ROSE GRABER

*A devotional book for
the new mother during the first
month following the birth
of her baby*

HERALD PRESS
SCOTTDALE, PENNSYLVANIA

International Standard Book Number 0-8361-1391-8
Library of Congress Catalog Card Number: 53-7585
Seventeenth Printing, 1970

To my own dear mother
who first revealed to me
the beauty of motherhood

Preface

Today you are a *mother*. Beside you lies a little soul, wrapped in the swaddling clothes of innocency, purity, love, and trust. Where he has come from, you do not really know; how you deserve him, you will never understand; what lies in store for him, only the future will reveal. In him is life which will survive the ages, and even now he is a part of things eternal, for Jesus said, "Of such is the kingdom of heaven."

All in all, you have had a momentous experience, and joy has been written into every chapter of it. There was personal joy, an unequaled thrill over the baby's first cry. There was family joy, for the coming of the new member draws parents closer together than ever before. There was spiritual joy, for you have co-operated with God your Maker in the wonderful creation of a new life.

Great moments in one's life are never without their special problems, though, and certainly new motherhood has its full share. You may have thought that you had fully prepared for the coming of the little basket-dweller, but there are many details which now require your constant attention. The *human* infant is the most helpless of all God's babies, and all the answers are not to be found in the baby book!

Doctors will tell you that while your strength is coming back, physical and glandular changes are taking place in your body which can affect your emotional life. And since one's spiritual life is so closely associated with one's physical and emotional well-being, you no doubt feel the need of the loving presence of God in a very special way at this time.

It is as a result of my own experience of new motherhood, with its accompanying joys and problems, that I have prepared this little book of *Meditations for the New Mother,* a collection of Scriptures, poetry, and devotional thoughts especially meaningful after the birth of a baby. My prayer is that the rich passages of the Word of God will not only inspire you during that first important month of your baby's life, but will continue to guide you in your lifelong task of motherhood.

Perhaps I should make an apology to mothers of baby girls. In o r d e r to avoid calling the baby "it," I had to use the word "he" throughout the book. However, I hope you will not have too much trouble substituting the words "she," "her," and "hers."

I wish to thank especially Mary Royer, Ph.D., Goshen College, Goshen, Indiana, and my husband, Virgil Brenneman, as well as many other friends for their kind help and encouragement in the completion of this book.

Iowa City, Iowa   HELEN GOOD BRENNEMAN

Contents

III. "Therefore . . . I have lent him to the Lord"

OUR RESPONSIBILITY TO THE CHILD

I. "For this child I prayed . . ."

THANKSGIVING FOR THE CHILD

"For this child I prayed; and the Lord hath given me my petition which I asked of him: therefore also I have lent him to the Lord; as long as he liveth he shall be lent to the Lord."

I Samuel 1:27, 28

The Fruit of Your Womb

"Lo, children are an heritage of the Lord:
And the fruit of the womb is his reward.
As arrows are in the hand of a mighty man;
So are children of the youth.
Happy is the man that hath his quiver full of them."

PSALM 127:3, 4, 5a

At the dawn of the world, in the morning of time, God looked down upon the beautiful earth which He had made and climaxed His creation by placing a man and a woman in the first home. Now life together for the world's first married couple must have been romantic and very happy, for they loved one another, and their garden-home was exquisitely furnished.

Yet God, in His wisdom, knew that two young people, however much in love, needed something to lift them above themselves and make their affection of a deeper, more lasting nature. Indeed, so great had been His satisfaction in creating this young couple that the Father, wishing to share His creative joy, commanded them to be fruitful, to multiply, and to replenish the earth.

Thus began family life on the earth, and so bearing and bringing up children has continued throughout the ages to be a tender and joyful experience. Thus it was several ages later when David, king and father, wrote of the happiness that comes with children, the heritage of the Lord. Thus it was that Jesus Himself took the babies of His day into His arms to bless them. And thus it is for *you*, today, New Mother, as you join hands with the mothers of the ages, praising the Lord your Maker for the fruit of your womb, your reward and heritage of the Lord, your new baby!

O God, my heavenly Father, I thank Thee with all my heart for the beautiful experience of motherhood and for the baby at my side. Just as Thou hast helped the mothers of all ages, guide me in my new task, bless my precious baby, and bless the baby's father in his love and concern for both of us. Amen.

· 15 ·

A MOTHER

God sought to give the sweetest thing
 In His almighty power
To earth; and deeply pondering
 What it should be, one hour
In fondest joy and love of heart
 Outweighing every other,
He moved the gates of heaven apart
 And gave to earth a mother.

AUTHOR UNKNOWN

A babe in a house is a wellspring of pleasure.

M. F. TOPPER

Hannah's Song

"And Hannah prayed, and said,
My heart rejoiceth in the Lord,
Mine horn is exalted in the Lord. . . .
There is none holy as the Lord:
For there is none beside thee:
Neither is there any rock like our God."

Read I Samuel 2:1-10.

Truly the story of Hannah is a woman's story; it is a mother's story. Our hearts beat sympathetically with the heart of this would-be mother who so much desired a child that "she wept, and did not eat." Can you not see her at the temple as "in bitterness of soul" she "prayed unto the Lord, and wept sore"? None of us who have felt that God-given hunger for motherhood and for the warmth of a baby in our arms would censure her for the agreement which she made with God. The Father Himself did not reprove her for it but answered her prayer, accepted her child, and used him mightily in His kingdom. And then, to end the story beautifully, He gave her three more sons and two daughters to bless her life and to make her home complete.

Little Samuel was a *wanted* child and his earliest years were filled with his mother's love. Moreover, Hannah did not forget the Lord when her prayer was answered, as so many do today. When her child was weaned, she took him to the temple, gave him to the Lord, and uttered a prayer that has come down to us through the ages. The prayer expresses joy in her God, victory over her difficulties, stability founded upon the Rock of her salvation, humility, strength, and justice.

Let us today follow Hannah's example as we, too, "praise the Lord for his goodness, and for his wonderful works to the children of men!"

O Lord, my refuge and my fortress, my rock, in whom I trust, I praise Thee for the protection of Thy wings and for the strength of Thy presence. I thank Thee also for laying this little child in my arms to love and to cherish. Help me, his mother, always to dwell under the shadow of the Almighty, in the secret place of the most High. Amen.

· 17 ·

HIS CRADLE

It rocked and rocked for joy,
This battered world,
When Mary's little boy
Up in it curled,
Despite its chill.
O may He fill
Today His chosen bed,
Through you and me,
Who love and help to spread
Simplicity.

HERBERT SEYMOUR HASTINGS

The Birth of Our Lord

"And the angel said unto her,

    Fear not, Mary: for thou hast found favour with God.

    And, behold, thou shalt conceive in thy womb,

      and bring forth a son,

      and shalt call his name Jesus. . . .

    And she brought forth her firstborn son,

      and wrapped him in swaddling clothes,

      and laid him in a manger."

Read Luke 2:1-7.

How strange it seems to us, as we lie in our comfortable beds, that the Lord of glory, who deserved the most luxurious cradle in all the world, should be born in a barn and cushion His downy head on a pillow of straw! How bumpy the ride must have seemed to Mary as she traveled, probably on the back of a donkey, all the way from Nazareth to Bethlehem! She may even have walked those hundred miles. Did she and Joseph understand the prophecy concerning Jesus' birthplace, or did they sometimes fear that the child might be born before they reached their destination?

The story is told of a little girl, in a well-to-do home, who said one day, "Mamma, I don't understand why, if God is so rich, He let His Son be born in a manger. Why didn't He buy Him a little bed like mine?"

We could speculate on the delivery in that unsanitary stable, the lack of an attendant physician, the simple layette which Mary had brought along from her home. But all these details are lost in the splendor of the occasion, beginning when the angel first told Mary that she was to bring forth the "Son of the Highest." The simplicity of the setting accentuates the beauty of the Child, the wonder of His coming, and the quiet worship of the first visitors who knelt at His feet. May we at this joyous time of our lives meditate on the birth of our Saviour, opening our hearts to Him as never before!

Father in heaven, who didst send Thine only Son to us as a little babe, I thank Thee for the miracle of birth. I thank Thee, too, that because a Saviour was born into this world, I can be "born again" into the kingdom of God. May the birth of my child remind me of Thy Son who came that I, believing on Him, might have life everlasting. Amen.

MATERNITY

Within the crib that stands beside my bed
A little form in sweet abandon lies
And as I bend above with misty eyes
I know how Mary's heart was comforted.

O world of Mothers! blest are we who know
The ecstasy—the deep God-given thrill
That Mary felt when all the earth was still
In that Judean starlight long ago!

ANNE P. L. FIELD

Mary's Song

"And Mary said,
> My soul doth magnify the Lord,
> And my spirit hath rejoiced in God my Saviour.
> For he hath regarded the low estate of his handmaiden:
> For, behold, from henceforth all generations shall call me blessed."

Read Luke 1:46-55.

When expectant mothers get together, there is always a great deal of hopeful, animated conversation. But the famous meeting of Mary, the mother of Jesus, and Elisabeth, the mother of John the Baptist, had more than the usual amount of excitement and joy. Filled with the Holy Spirit, Elisabeth shouted,
> "Blessed are you among women,
> And blessed is your child! . . .
> For as soon as your greeting reached my ears,
> The baby leaped for joy within me!" *(Williams Translation)*

Mary's Magnificat of thanksgiving is much like the song of Hannah. Mary, too, makes the occasion one of praise to God for His greatness, His holiness, His mercy, His strength, and His justice. In her humility she wonders at the Almighty's choice of a lowly handmaiden such as herself to be forever blessed among women.

If Mary's heart were so filled with praise before the Lord Jesus was born, can you imagine her joy when at last God Incarnate lay in her arms as a tiny babe? After the shepherds had returned to their fields, Luke tells us that "Mary kept all these things, and pondered them in her heart." Hers must have been a quiet, devout personality, for she discreetly meditated upon the momentous events of her days, looking to God for strength to face her new responsibilities.

Our task is second only to Mary's, and the God of our strength is the same loving Father who watched over the divine infant two thousand years ago. Let us, like Mary, face the future with praise, confidence, and unconquerable faith in our God.

My Father and my God, my heart has thrilled over the praise and thanksgiving of Mary, Jesus' mother. I cannot find words to express my joy as she did, but Thou knowest what is in my heart. I give Thee my wordless thanks and ask of Thee courage for the days and nights ahead. Amen.

COMETH THE CHILD

Fresh from the hand of the Father
  New from His latest creating
Clean from Love's all-golden weather
  To a bleak climate of hating
To the old failures of ages
  To a worn book, a stale story
Onto Earth's intricate pages
  Cometh the child in his glory.

Through him our purpose, once restive
  Focuses full upon duty;
Through him our joy gains refining,
  We through his eyes see new beauty.
Through him our haughty hearts crumble,
  The hills and the vales are made even;
Through him our proud souls made simple
  Find grace at the threshold of heaven.

MIRIAM SIEBER LIND

Elisabeth's Preparation

"And they were both righteous before God,
Walking in all the commandments and ordinances of
the Lord blameless."

Read Luke 1:5-17.

God, who "seeth not as man seeth . . . but . . . looketh on the heart," did not choose men and women of great worldly influence to take part in the events surrounding the birth of our Saviour. Instead He selected poor, humble, ordinary folks, people who were "walking in all the commandments and ordinances of the Lord blameless." And what better qualification for parenthood can we find than a pious, God-fearing heart such as God saw in Zacharias and Elisabeth?

Most of the account of the birth of John the Baptist describes the experiences of Zacharias, his initial sin of doubt and his final triumph of faith. But of Elisabeth we read only of her joy that the Lord had finally taken away her reproach and had answered her prayer. We see her faith, her humility, and her obedience in the naming and training of her son. What a commentary on her character, that the angel Gabriel could send the youthful Mary to Elisabeth to be strengthened in courage and in faith!

Because of her faithfulness to God, Elisabeth was able to carry out the plan which the heavenly Father had for her, and her son "continued to grow and to gain strength in the Spirit" (Luke 1:80, Williams translation).

Although the purpose of the little life at our side has not been announced to us by angels, God just as surely has a plan for him as He did for John the Baptist. Thus our song of thanksgiving should be accompanied by a prayer for inward purity, that we, too, may be prepared to carry out God's will in the training of our child.

I see, dear God, that the most important preparation for me in my duties as a mother is to live a righteous, blameless life as an example to my child. Since I cannot do this in my own strength, come into my heart and abide there. Strengthen my inner self with the presence of Thy Spirit. In Jesus' name I ask this. Amen.

· 23 ·

They say that man is mighty,
  He governs land and sea,
He wields a mighty scepter
  O'er lesser powers than he;

But mightier power and stronger
  Man from his throne has hurled,
For the hand that rocks the cradle
  Is the hand that rules the world.

W. R. WALLACE

An ounce of mother is worth a pound of clergy.

SPANISH PROVERB

Jochebed's Privilege

> "And the woman conceived, and bare a son: and when she saw him that he was a goodly child, she hid him three months. And when she could not longer hide him, she took for him an ark . . . and put the child therein; and she laid it in the flags by the river's brink."

Read Exodus 2:1-10.

Little Moses was born in troublesome times, in an age when Hebrew mothers could rightly feel insecure about the future of their infant sons. So intent was Pharaoh on subduing the Jewish people, that he used every horrible method in his power to halt the increase of this minority group in his land.

We do not know much about Jochebed, Moses' mother, but we can see that she must have been endowed with a generous portion of motherly wisdom and guided by a higher power. For she actually carried out a plan which not only saved the life of her baby, but established him in the palace of the monarch who sought to destroy him.

When Moses was born, his mother was probably too busy keeping him hidden from the authorities to write a song of thanksgiving such as Hannah and Elisabeth did. But when he was three months old how she must have rejoiced! God, in His providence, had given her the privilege of caring for her son and training him in ways of righteousness for a lifetime of service. Although Jochebed did not know it then, her little son was one day to become a leader of God's people, forever remembered for his faith and obedience to God.

Certainly God is honored by our words of praise and thanksgiving, but He wants something more of us. He wants us to show our gratitude to Him by bringing up sons and daughters who, like Moses, "refuse to be called the son of Pharaoh's daughter; choosing rather to suffer affliction with the people of God, than to enjoy the pleasures of sin for a season" (Hebrews 11:24, 25).

Gracious Father, I thank Thee for the example of Jochebed, one of the great mothers of all time. If Thou couldst deliver her from such a great danger, certainly Thou canst guide me in the perplexing problems of caring for my baby. For I, too, want to take good care of my child and train him for Thy service. Amen.

THE NEW BABY

"How funny and red!"
  That's what they said.
"Why, there's nothing but fuzz
  On top of his head."
And they lifted the covers
  To look at his feet.
"Oh, how tiny and wrinkled
  And red as a beet!"
And I heard them whispering
  Behind my back,
"Did you ever think
  He would look like that,
All wrinkled and red
  Like a baby bird?"
Of course they didn't
  Know that I heard.
But I had to smile
  When the baby was fed
To see how fast
  They lined up by his bed,
And in spite of the fact
  He was wrinkled and thin,
They all begged for a turn
  At holding him.

OSIE HERTZLER ZIEGLER

Family Joy

"God setteth the solitary in families. . . ."

PSALM 68:6

"Thy wife shall be as a fruitful vine
  by the sides of thine house:
  thy children like olive plants
  round about thy table."

PSALM 128:3

In a day when family life is disintegrating, when selfishness breaks up homes and brings unwanted children into the world, how refreshing and how stabilizing is our never-changing God and His divine institution, the Christian home!

According to Psalm 128, it is the man that "feareth the Lord; that walketh in his ways," who finds in his wife and children the deepest and finest satisfaction. Psalm 127 says, "Happy is the man that hath his quiver full of them [children]." Of course, this "quiverful" joy of which the psalmist speaks is not selfish parental pride, which takes personal glory for a God-given gift. While "quiverful" joy does not express itself in boasting about one's children, it does bring with it, however, a wholesome type of self-respect. For the psalmist says, "They shall not be ashamed, but they shall speak with the enemies in the gate."

The woman who obeys God's call to motherhood is acting in accordance with the plan of an all-knowing God for her life. The psalmist pictures her here as a beautiful, fruitful vine, and the writer of the Proverbs says that her value is far above rubies. In motherhood, as in all areas of life, living in the will of God brings inner peace, delightful experiences, and lasting satisfaction in addition to the daily round of problems, trials, and lessons, hard-learned.

Dear Father of fathers and mothers, I thank Thee for establishing the home as a place where we can share life's most beautiful relationships. I thank Thee for making me a woman, a wife, and a mother. May I be worthy of this call; may I make my home a joyous place. In Jesus' name. Amen.

A tired old doctor died today, and a baby boy was born—
A little new soul that was pink and frail,
    and a soul that was gray and worn.
And—halfway here and halfway there
On a white, high hill of shining air—
They met and passed and paused to speak
    in the flushed and hearty dawn.

The man looked down at the soft, small thing,
    with wise and weary eyes;
And the little chap stared back at him,
    with startled, scared surmise,
And then he shook his downy head—
"I think I won't be born," he said;
"You are too gray and sad!" And he shrank
    from the pathway down the skies.

But the tired old doctor roused once more
    at the battle-cry of birth,
And there was memory in his look, of grief
    and toil and mirth.
"Go on!" he said. "It's good—and bad:
It's hard! Go on! It's ours, my lad."
And he stood and urged him out of sight,
    down to the waiting earth.

HAROLD FRANCIS BRANCH

An Even Greater Joy

"A woman when she is in travail hath sorrow, because her hour is come: but as soon as she is delivered of the child, she remembereth no more the anguish, for joy that a man is born into the world. And ye now therefore have sorrow: but I will see you again, and your heart shall rejoice, and your joy no man taketh from you."

JOHN 16:21, 22

These comforting words, which break forth with fresh meaning to the mother of a newborn baby, were spoken by our Lord to His bewildered disciples just before He left them to be with His Father. With this vivid illustration Jesus showed how the difficulties of true Christian discipleship will one day be swallowed up in everlasting happiness.

They sat dejected around their Master, those eleven disciples, wishing that He would tell of their union with Him, instead of talking about leaving for some faraway place. If only He would speak to them more plainly! They could not understand what He meant by, "A little while, and ye behold me no more; and again a little while, and ye shall see me." The strange mixture of sorrow and joy, of suffering and comfort, of trouble and peace, puzzled them deeply.

Not until after Jesus rose from His grave, went up into heaven, and poured out His Holy Spirit did the disciples fully understand, "In the world ye shall have tribulation: but be of good cheer; I have overcome the world." The Comforter *did* come and Jesus' prayer for His followers was answered with spiritual power that continued bearing fruit through the centuries.

Bringing the lesson back to us, we have already forgotten those anxious hours of labor before our baby came, in the tremendous satisfaction that he is here. How much more quickly we will forget life's problems when eternity suddenly ushers us into the long-awaited presence of our Lord Jesus Christ!

O Christ, we thank Thee for explaining the great truths of the kingdom in words we can all understand. We thank Thee for earthly joys that remind us of the pleasures of eternity with Thee. May I, to-day, sit in heavenly places in Thee, that in ages to come I may enjoy the exceeding riches of Thy grace in heaven itself. In Thy name I pray. Amen.

A TRIBUTE TO CHILDHOOD

When God made the child He began early in the morning. He watched the golden hues of the rising day chasing away the darkness, and He chose the azure of the opening heavens for the color of childhood's eyes, the crimson of the clouds to paint its cheeks, and the gold of the morning for its flowing tresses. He listened to the song of the birds as they sang and warbled and whispered, and strung childhood's harp with notes now soft and low—now sweet and strong.

He saw little lambs among the flock romp and play and skip, and He put play into childhood's heart. He saw the silvery brook and listened to its music and He made the laughter of the child like the ripple of the brook. He saw angels of light as upon the wings of love they hastened to holy duty, and He formed the child's heart in purity and love.

And having made the child, He sent it out to bring joy into the home, laughter on the green and gladness everywhere. He sent it into the home and said to the parents, "Nourish and bring up this child for me." He sent it to the church and said, "Teach it my love and my laws." He sent it to the state and said, "Deal tenderly with it and it will bless and not curse you." He sent it to the nation and said, "Be good to the child. It is thy greatest asset and thy hope."

GEORGE W. RIDEOUT

The Perfect Gift

"Every good and every perfect gift is from above, and cometh down from the Father of lights, with whom is no variableness, neither shadow of turning."

JAMES 1:17

A friend of ours, charmed by the joys of first parenthood, wrote us in a letter, "I still wonder at what age parents may begin to take credit for such good behavior; so far the goodness of the gift reflects the greater goodness of the Giver." We all agree that there is no age when *we* can take credit for the miracle of love which is now ours, for the gift is absolutely unmerited and the glory belongs to the King of glory!

Our wiggly little bundle came at Christmas time, reminding us in a special way that babies are remarkable gifts. Certainly no gift had ever brought with it such demands upon our time, energy, and pocket-book. But neither had any previous Christmas present brought eternal significance. A divinely planned blend of both our personalities, he was at the same time a new and living soul. Scarcely aware of anything beyond himself and his needs, he came to us with an amazing capacity for love, a love which developed and matured as he was loved by other people and learned about the love of God. And most significant of all, this gift was created by God Himself, in His own image and for His own glory. Ours for today, he is God's for eternity.

"What shall I render unto the Lord
  for all his benefits toward me?
I will take the cup of salvation,
  and call upon the name of the Lord.
I will pay my vows unto the Lord now
  in the presence of all his people."

THE PSALMIST (PSALM 116:12-14)

· 31 ·

THE MOTHER'S HYMN

Lord who ordainest for mankind
  Benignant toils and tender cares,
We thank Thee for the ties that bind
  The mother to the child she bears.

We thank Thee for the hopes that rise
  Within her heart, as, day by day,
The dawning soul, from those young eyes,
  Looks with a clearer, steadier ray.

And graieful for the blessing given
  With that dear infant on her knee,
She trains the eye to look to heaven,
  The voice to lisp a prayer to Thee.

Such thanks the blessed Mary gave
  When from her lap the Holy Child,
Sent from on high to seek and save
  The lost of earth, looked up and smiled.

All-Gracious! grant to those who bear
  A mother's charge, the strength and light
To guide the feet that own their care
  In ways of Love and Truth and Right.

WILLIAM CULLEN BRYANT

A Psalm of Thanksgiving

"Make a joyful noise unto the Lord, all ye lands.
Serve the Lord with gladness:
Come before his presence with singing.
Know ye that the Lord he is God:
It is he that hath made us, and not we ourselves;
We are his people, and the sheep of his pasture.

"Enter into his gates with thanksgiving,
And into his courts with praise:
Be thankful unto him, and bless his name.
For the Lord is good; his mercy is everlasting;
And his truth endureth to all generations."

THE PSALMIST (PSALM 100)

II. "The Lord hath given me my petition . . ."

MEDITATIONS ON THE CHILD

TO A CHILD I KNOW

Dear little child with eyes
  Like violets glowing,
And face all dimpled with
  Enchanting smile,
You have a beauty which is
  Innocently flowing
Unhindered yet by any
  Thought of guile.
Your soul is breathing
  Peaceful as a flower,
And loving me keeps me
  In touch with love,
Before the world steps in
  I prize each precious hour,
That lifts my soul through you
  To God above.

J. M. BALLANTYNE

As a Little Child

"A little child shall lead them."

ISAIAH 11:6b

"Out of the mouth of babes and sucklings thou hast perfected praise." MATTHEW 21:16

"And he took a child, and set him in the midst of them."

MARK 9:36

To Jesus' most intimate earthly friends, the twelve disciples, some of His words and actions were surely hard to understand. Although He was the greatest man who ever lived, the Son of the Highest, He told them that He had not come to save His life but to lose it. He came as a servant, not to be ministered unto, but to minister.

Not long after Jesus said, "If any man will come after me, let him deny himself," these poor, human disciples got into a foolish argument.

"I think *I* will be the greatest in the kingdom of heaven," was in essence what each one declared, giving no doubt his own convincing reasons.

How discouraging to the Lord Jesus, who had been trying to help them see what the *real* kingdom of God was like! But He did not rebuke them harshly. "If anyone wants to be the first, he must be the last of all and the servant of all" (Mark 9:35, Williams translation).

Then He gave them an object lesson they were not soon to forget. Drawing a little child to His bosom, He told them that if they were to enter the kingdom *at all*, they would have to become as little children. And if they were to become truly great, they must be willing to treat even little children as they would treat Him, their Lord.

It is easy to criticize those early followers, but how often we, too, are *childish* rather than *childlike*. How grateful we can be that God has set a little child in *our* midst, a little example of the simple virtues of innocence, meekness, trust, forgiveness, and love.

O Lord, Thou hast searched me and known me. Thou knowest that many times I am not childlike in spirit, but childish and selfish. Teach me, by observing my own small baby, some of the spiritual qualities Thou wouldst have me possess. Amen.

· 37 ·

"Suffer that little children come to Me,
Forbid them not." Emboldened by His words,
The mothers onward press; but, finding vain
The attempt to reach the Lord, they trust their babe
To strangers' hands; the innocents, alarmed
Amid the throng of faces all unknown,
Shrink, trembling, till their wandering eyes discern
The countenance of Jesus, beaming love
And pity; eager then they stretch their arms,
And, cowering, lay their heads upon His breast.

JAMES GRAHAME

The Child and the Christ

"Suffer the little children to come unto me, and forbid them not: for of such is the kingdom of God. . . . Whosoever shall not receive the kingdom of God as a little child, he shall not enter therein. And he took them up in his arms, put his hands upon them, and blessed them."

MARK 10:14, 15, 16

Even though Jesus had told the disciples how valuable little children were to Him, how every child's angel has access to the Father's throne, yet Christ's first kindergarten class was almost sent away from Him by those well-meaning friends of His. Jesus said, "Stop sending them away. The kingdom belongs to little children."

Wouldn't we have enjoyed crowding near Him with our babies, hearing His soft voice call them by name, watching Him caress them? What Jesus said to the children we do not know, but we can be sure He neither talked down to them nor did He speak above their heads. I like to picture Christ smiling with the children; He did not tease them nor laugh at them as some people are inclined to do. Taking them up in His arms, He simply loved them, laying the same kind hand on their heads that had brought strength and healing to so many.

Most parents are eager to bring their children to Jesus. But how often do their own hearts crave His fellowship? It has been said that little children respond more easily to Christian teaching than older people because of their rare combination of curiosity and confidence, their eagerness to learn and their willingness to believe. Are we as mothers also ready to sit at the feet of Jesus, drinking in His life-giving words along with our children? We can keep on learning about God and His universe while we teach our children; while we watch Him bless our babies, we, too, can worship at His feet, and be blessed.

Just as the mothers long ago, dear Christ, didst bring their little ones to Thee for Thy blessing, so I bring my baby to Thee today. Take him up in Thy everlasting arms and love him, I pray. And help me always to come to Thee for blessing and inspiration. In Thy name I ask these special favors. Amen.

HE TEACHES YOU

He's greater far, that little child, than you;
The very child you teach, he teaches you.
  You teach him to be Christlike, but have you
  Forgotten he already is, far more than you?
  You teach him right from wrong, and yet it's he,
  Not you, whose conscience is more clear and free.
  You teach him trust in God, but can't you see
  That it is you who lack trust more than he?
  For you find doubt and reason in your way
  While he in simple faith believes straightway.
  You teach him to forgive, but don't you know
  That he forgives in half the time you do?
  And he, when he forgives, at once forgets;
  But you? You struggle long with grudge and debts.
  You try to teach him love. You can't. You cry,
  "My child, you are the teacher, and not I!"
So learn from him, be like him, you who teach.
You must, Christ says, if heaven you would reach.

IDA BOYER BONTRAGER

The Child Teaches Us Humility

"Whosoever therefore shall humble himself as this little child, the same is greatest in the kingdom of heaven."

MATTHEW 18:4

If thou, O daughter of the King, wouldst be truly humble, consider the baby which the Lord hath bestowed upon thee!

Paul once said to Timothy, "For we brought nothing into this world, and it is certain we can carry nothing out." If ever anyone came to your house with an empty suitcase, your baby did. Aside from those physical and mental capacities waiting to be developed as part of his personality, your baby came to this world empty-handed.

He came without ambition or reputation. Indeed, he can afford to be himself at all times; he never puts on a front. That word "innocence" describes how completely without worldly wisdom your little one is.

Your baby entered this world without a resentment of any kind, and it will be a long time before he learns to hold a grudge or carry ill will around on his little shoulders. May he never learn! He is a twig unbent, totally bereft of any prejudices. Humble, sincere learner that he is, he is completely teachable.

The baby enters this universe without anxiety. If he has any "fears" at all, they are not the foolish, complicated variety that haunt our grown-up lives. The baby does not trouble himself about where his next meal will come from nor what will happen to him tomorrow.

Probably the outstanding lesson Jesus wanted us to learn from the child is the lesson of *humility,* fundamental to all the other Christian graces.

To humble ourselves as a little child, we must lay aside ambition and reputation, resentments and prejudices, anxieties and materialistic concerns of this life. Stripped of the veneer of sophistication which hides our genuine selves, we must let the honest, sincere, trustful, loving, forgiving, learning child live within us.

For, "Whosoever shall not receive the kingdom of God as a little child shall in no wise enter therein."

I thank thee, O Father, Lord of heaven and earth, because thou hast hid these things from the wise and prudent, and hast revealed them unto babes (A prayer of Jesus, as recorded in Matthew 11:25).

· 41 ·

TRUST IN GOD

The child leans on its parent's breast,
Leaves there its cares and is at rest;
The bird sits singing by his nest,
  And tells aloud
His trust in God, and so is blest
  'Neath every cloud.

He has no store, he sows no seed;
Yet sings aloud, and doth not heed;
By flowing stream or grassy mead,
  He sings to shame
Men, who forget, in fear of need,
  A Father's name.

The heart that trusts for ever sings,
And feels as light as it had wings;
A well of peace within it springs;
  Come good or ill.
Whate'er today, tomorrow, brings,
  It is His will.

ISAAC WILLIAMS

The Child Teaches Us Trust

"If ye then, being evil, know how to give good gifts unto your children, how much more shall your Father which is in heaven give good things to them that ask him?"

Read Matthew 7:7-11.

When my baby was born and I saw how completely helpless and dependent he was upon me, I was frightened, for I knew my own limitations and lack of experience. It was fortunate that the baby was ignorant of his mother's woeful inexperience: otherwise he never could have slept so sweetly in his little basket!

The utter dependence of a new baby upon his mother has often been used to illustrate the helpless state in which we find ourselves, as children of our Father in heaven. Just as a mother watches over her child with unfailing love, regardless of his inability to express his needs in words and sentences, so the loving father-heart of God is sensitive to our every cry. Our Father knows what things we have need of even before we ask Him. Jesus told us that Himself.

As a child grows older, his trust in his parents becomes a more intelligent response. He sees them as people who express their love for him in many little ways. Despite a painful trip to the dentist, a dose of foul-tasting medicine, or an occasional spanking, the child knows his parents love him.

Sometimes we as Christians are faced with situations which try us and for which we, like Job, can see no reason.

Our trust in God, to be really perfect and childlike, must accept the higher wisdom of His love in difficult situations as well as when things are going our way. Paul's advice to the Philippians on prayerful trust is "good for what ails us" today. Let's put it to practice!

"Be careful for nothing; but in every thing by prayer and supplication with thanksgiving let your requests be made known unto God.

"And the peace of God, which passeth all understanding, shall keep your hearts and minds through Christ Jesus."

PHILIPPIANS 4:6, 7

My loving Father in heaven, how glad I am that I can relax in the thought of Thy tender concern for me. Just as my baby trusts in me completely, so I rest in the security of Thy love. Give me the inner peace that manifests itself in strength and poise. In the name of Thy Son I ask this. Amen.

· 43 ·

SAVIOUR, TEACH ME DAY BY DAY

Saviour, teach me day by day
Love's sweet lesson to obey;
Sweeter lesson cannot be:
Loving Him who first loved me.

With a childlike heart of love,
At Thy bidding may I move,
Prompt to serve and follow Thee—
Loving Him who first loved me.

JANE E. LEESON

The Child Teaches Us the Love of the Father

"As one whom his mother comforteth, so will I comfort you." ISAIAH 66:13a

"Like as a father pitieth his children, so the Lord pitieth them that fear him." PSALM 103:13

A young mother, noticing that the baby of the family was not benefiting from her Bible story hour with the older children, decided that she would show him the love of the heavenly Father in a way he could better understand—by taking him in her arms and rocking him. As she sat thus meditating and cuddling him, her own spiritual life was enriched and strengthened.

A dear old disciple of Christ, eighty-nine years of age, once said that although he was the fifteenth child in his family, he always believed that his mother loved him best of all. During the many years that followed his babyhood, the memory of that loving Christian mother pointed him to a heavenly Father who comforts like a mother and pities as an earthly father.

As much as we love our babies, we know that God the Father loves us with a more perfect love. We are such imperfect symbols of God's parental affection, for our Father is never annoyed when we cry. He is never physically tired. He never slumbers nor sleeps. He watches over us with even deeper concern than we have for our own little sleepers. How warm, how secure, how comforting it is to have a God like that!

One evening, as I sat feeding my baby, he suddenly stopped eating, laid his head against my shoulder, and touching my cheek with his chubby little hand, said, "Ah, Ah." As I pondered this little note of endearment, I came to the conclusion that true worship is probably nothing more than touching the kind cheek of the heavenly Father and whispering, "Ah, Ah, dear Father."

Oh, that my worship of Thee, dear God, would be as free and spontaneous as the love of a little child for his mother. Help me to nurture my babe in such a tender way that when we tell him of Thy love, he will understand and love Thee in response. Amen.

FAITH OF OUR MOTHERS

Faith of our mothers, living yet
  In cradle song and bedtime prayer,
In nursery love and fireside lore,
  Thy presence still pervades the air.
Faith of our mothers, living faith,
We will be true to thee till death.

Faith of our mothers, lavish faith,
  The fount of childhood's trust and grace,
O may thy consecration prove
  The wellspring of a nobler race.
Faith of our mothers, lavish faith,
We will be true to thee till death.

Faith of our mothers, guiding faith,
  For youthful longings—youthful doubts,
How blurred our vision, blind our way,
  Thy providential care without.
Faith of our mothers, guiding faith,
We will be true to thee till death.

Faith of our mothers, Christian faith,
  In truth beyond our man-made creeds,
Still serve the home and save the church,
  And breathe thy spirit through our deeds.
Faith of our mothers, Christian faith,
We will be true to thee till death.

ARTHUR B. PATTEN

The Child Our Imitator

"When I call to remembrance the unfeigned faith that is in thee, which dwelt first in thy grandmother Lois, and thy mother Eunice; and I am persuaded that in thee also."

II TIMOTHY 1:5

"When I grow up I want to be just like Mother (or Daddy)," is a more sobering statement than we perhaps think. For children are little imitators, every one of them, and they are going to imitate and grow to be like those with whom they live. The story is told of a little girl who was heard screeching at her dolls. When her mother asked the reason, she replied that she was playing "Mamma."

There are many vital habits which the child picks up unconsciously from his parents—little mannerisms, polite or rude manners, a sunny or a grouchy disposition, neat or slovenly appearance, good or bad attitudes, words, and actions.

Seeing his own faults and virtues "on parade" in his children has a rather startling effect on the average parent. Joseph Joubert, in the year 1842, expressed a great truth when he said, "Children need models more than they need critics." Children are quick to notice if we preach one thing and practice another in our everyday life. Nor can we hide unkind attitudes or other inconsistencies, thinking that our children will not see our real selves.

The Apostle Paul told his followers, "Be ye followers of me, even as I also am of Christ." Can we sincerely ask our little ones to follow us as *we* follow Christ? Are we passing on to them our strong faith, manifested in our every word and action?

I tried to lead a child through play
To grow more Christlike every day
And I myself became that way.

MABEL NIEDERMEYER McCAW

Dear Christ, this tiny baby, now so unconscious of all that is going on about him, will soon be watching and imitating the things I do. May I so closely imitate Thee that I will not need to fear my influence on his young life. Conform me, O Christ, to Thine own image, that my children may see the beauty of Jesus in me. Amen.

· 47 ·

I WOULD BE TRUE

I would be true, for there are those who trust me;
    I would be pure, for there are those who care;
I would be strong, for there is much to suffer;
    I would be brave, for there is much to dare.

I would be friend of all—the foe, the friendless;
    I would be giving, and forget the gift;
I would be humble, for I know my weakness;
    I would look up, and live, and love, and lift.

HOWARD ARNOLD WALTER

The Child Our Challenge to Pure Living

"Create in me a clean heart, O God; and renew a
right spirit within me."   PSALM 51:10

Have you ever cuddled your baby to your breast and said to him, perhaps not aloud, "You dear, innocent little soul, what a wretched old world I've brought you into"? I have. But I've gotten over worrying about what will become of him in the far-flung years of the future. For the most formative period of his life are those years with me before he ever faces that dubious, unreliable character, John Q. Public.

While my little fellow is still tagging on to the hem of my garment, he is going to be getting his basic training in life. As we noticed yesterday, he's going to imitate me, to gradually imbibe my actions and reactions, my habits and attitudes. This calls for scrupulous self-examination on my part and daily cleansing at the cross of Christ. What a challenge to pure living is the unstained life of a little child!

But how do we fit the devotional life into our busy mother schedules? When we are consciously walking with God, we are surprised at our many opportunities for informal fellowship with Him. Those pleasant periods when nursing or rocking our babies can well be used for meditation on a spiritual truth we need at the moment, for give-and-take conversation with the Lord, for thanksgiving and praise. We can memorize hymns as we iron; we can paste a precious Scripture above the kitchen sink. We can bring such big-little things to God as the formula we are mixing or the baby's colic.

The unblemished life of a newborn babe does indeed have a purifying influence on the lives of Christian parents. And it is only by keeping our own hearts and minds centered on the Lord Jesus Christ, that we will be able to lead our children into "whatsoever things are true . . . honest . . . just . . . pure . . . lovely . . . of good report."

Dear Jesus, I thank Thee that Thou art interested in every detail of my life. Help me to worship Thee as I go about my daily routine. Give me the grace to live above petty irritations and fretful worries. And when I fail, create in me a clean heart, O God, and renew a right spirit within me. Amen.

· 49 ·

TIME-HONORED TRUTH

The statement may seem very trite,
 It has been said so often,
That babies have been sent from heav'n
 Our calloused hearts to soften.

But though the story may be old,
 It's changed no jot or tittle,
The baby is God's messenger
 E'en though he is so little.

And so I feel the aged truth
 Needs no fresh interpretation—
A baby's face is heaven's grace
 To any generation.

HELEN GOOD BRENNEMAN

The Child, Preserver of Life Values

"Hear, ye children, the instruction of a father,
  and attend to know understanding.
For I give you good doctrine, forsake ye not my law.
For I was my father's son, tender and only beloved
  in the sight of my mother.
He taught me also, and said unto me,
Let thine heart retain my words:
Keep my commandments, and live."

PROVERBS 4:1-4

In the days when the great-grandchildren of the aged Joseph were brought to his knees to be blessed, people considered it a high privilege to become acquainted with and to influence one's posterity. In Psalm 128:6 we read, "Yea, thou shalt see thy children's children, and peace upon Israel," a promise made to the man who feared the Lord. Proverbs 17:6 states, "Children's children are the crown of old men; and the glory of children are their fathers."

One day my husband and I were invited as guests to a large family reunion. The carry-in dinner was spread on long tables; the picnic grounds were dotted with cousins of every age and size. To our surprise we were informed that all these people, despite their differences in personality and appearance, were by birth or marriage direct descendants of one couple just a few generations back. We could only wonder what a family reunion several years hence would reveal in our own children and our children's children. Will our Christian nurture be strong and winsome enough to bear fruit in future generations? What ideals will we plant in our young, what values will we teach as important?

In our children we have an opportunity to live again, for the child is a preserver of our life values; thus may we strive for the highest goals in life, as did one minister who said, "If we cannot leave a single dollar to our children, let us give them the more important heritage of godly Christian parents."

Gracious God, I thank Thee for strong family ties that bind us together with those we love. I thank Thee for my own parents and grandparents who taught me principles of right living. Bless the baby's grandparents, give wisdom to us his parents, and help us all to inspire him to love and follow Thee. Amen.

· 51 ·

Not in the clamor of the crowded street,
Not in the shouts and plaudits of the throng,
But in ourselves are triumph and defeat.

HENRY WADSWORTH LONGFELLOW

"He that ruleth his spirit [is better] than he that taketh
a city." PROVERBS 16:32b

The Child an Individual

"And the Lord God formed man of the dust of the ground, and breathed into his nostrils the breath of life; and man became a living soul." GENESIS 2:7

Before we close the section of meditations on the child and his meaning to us, we must consider him in his own right, as a new and separate individual. Though he may look like Uncle John and have ears like his mother's side of the family, God has given him a personality all his own, one which like a bud will gradually unfold before our wondering eyes.

Alta Mae Erb, in her book on *The Christian Nurture of Children,* says that a child's personality is determined by: his inherited possibilities, his physical body, his surroundings, his own individual self, and salvation of this self through Christ. And strange as it may seem, the first six months of one's life are very significant, for the many influences on a child's personality begin operating powerfully when he is still a babe-in-arms.

To ignore the rights of a little child as a person is unkind and unjust. He is not a grownup in miniature form and dare not be treated as such. His personality needs to be respected, and we need to build solid character and lofty ideals upon his own particular characteristics and needs. Although we cannot preach sermons to him when he is only three weeks old, we can start developing the text of our lifetime sermon: love. For the love of two emotionally mature Christian parents is our baby's greatest need.

Delicate plants require patient, skillful, loving care. How much more does the sensitive personality of a little child need the sunshine of our love and the careful nurture of sympathizing parents. What a privilege and what a *responsibility* it is for us to guard the development of an immortal soul!

Dear God, in view of all that is expected of a mother, I would feel most inadequate were not my hand in Thine. I thank Thee for entrusting me with a living soul. Help me to bring out the best that is in him, teaching him above all things to live, move, and have his being in Thee. In Jesus' name. Amen.

THE CHILD'S APPEAL

I am the Child.
All the world waits for my coming.
All the earth watches with interest to see what I shall become.
Civilization hangs in the balance,
For what I am, the world of tomorrow will be.

I am the Child.
I have come into your world, about which I know nothing.
Why I came I know not;
How I came I know not.
I am curious; I am interested.

I am the Child.
You hold in your hand my destiny.
You determine, largely, whether I shall succeed or fail.
Give me, I pray you, those things that make for happiness.
Train me, I beg you, that I may be a blessing to the world.

MAMIE GENE COLE

The Child Our Trust

"Therefore let no man glory in men. For all things are yours . . . the world . . . life . . . death . . . things present . . . things to come; all are yours; and ye are Christ's; and Christ is God's." I CORINTHIANS 3:21-23

Of all the challenging truths which we, like Mary, have pondered in our hearts since our baby's birth, our small part in creating an ever-lasting soul is surely the most awe-inspiring. Masefield states the majesty of giving birth to a child in the words:

"And he who gives a child a treat
Makes joy-bells ring in Heaven's street,
And he who gives a child a home
Builds palaces in Kingdom come,
And she who gives a baby birth
Brings Saviour Christ again to Earth."*

One evening my husband and I called in the home of new parents and found them sitting blissfully in their living room, watching the sleeping infant with quiet satisfaction. "Such a sweet little life God has given us to care for," the mother whispered. "Just think, he is really not ours, but God's."

I like to think of the security of a baby born in a Christian home. In a way, we can call the baby our own, but since we are Christ's and Christ is God's, the baby ultimately belongs to Him. How secure our children are in the close relationship of God's "family tree": baby, mother, father, Christ, God!

Thus, as we meditate upon our child we think of him as our *trust,* the one whom God has given us in stewardship to bring up for Him. Like the mother of Samson we cry at this point, "Teach us what we shall do unto the child. . . ." And how ready our heavenly Father is to do just that!

I gladly take, kind Father, this trust which Thou hast bestowed upon me. I thank Thee for the lovely dependence of a baby upon his parents, of one parent upon the other, and of both parents upon Thee. Therefore I do not take the responsibilities of motherhood upon my own shoulders alone. In Thee I go forward with confidence. Amen.

*John Masefield, *The Everlasting Mercy*

III. "Therefore also I have lent him to the Lord . . ."

OUR RESPONSIBILITY TO THE CHILD

FOR MATTHEW

Dear Little One,
Our newest, tenderest son,
What world we brought you to, we cannot know.

Neither did Hannah know
As on her happy heart sweet Samuel lay
A very Yes of God.

Neither did Eunice know
As, prattling prayers, the tiny Timothy stood
Within her circling arms.

Nor did the saintly Monica foresee
If her Augustine's world should thrive or split;

And that unique Susannah, tutoring
Young John, small Charles,
She knew no more than they . . .

Than I. But I do know,
As faith-filled they too knew,
That if your times be anguished or be still
It is God's will
That you should live therein to His high praise.

And so I singing hold you to myself.
In strong sweet faith I sing;
Our little son,
Dear, newest, tenderest One.

MIRIAM SIEBER LIND

Dedicating and Educating

"Therefore . . . I have lent him to the Lord."
I SAMUEL 1:28

We all admire the woman Hannah, who prayed for Samuel, thanked God for his coming, and dedicated him to Jehovah, making what seems to us a supreme sacrifice. At the same time we wonder what we have in common with her experience, for we keep our children, do we not? We do not take them to a temple and give them to an old man to take care of. That was what God asked of Hannah, but He asks us not only to *dedicate* but also to *educate* our children.

Exactly how long Hannah had her son with her we do not know, but women those days did not wean their children as early as we do now. On the basis of Jewish customs some Bible students believe that she took Samuel to the temple only for a visit during his infancy and then left him there when he was six years old. Be that as it may, after she had placed his dimpled hand in the wrinkled one of Eli, Hannah's task was done, except for her trip each year to take him the new coat she had made so carefully for him.

There probably isn't one of us who would want to trade places with Hannah. Yet, when we dedicate our babies to the Lord we, too, make a sobering commitment. He may take them home to be with Him if it is His will; if He leaves them with us we will lead them in paths of righteousness, trusting that they will sometime dedicate their *own* young lives to His service.

A look at the One to whom we dedicate, however, takes away any haunting dread of releasing to the Lord what seems to be ours. And one look at Him who "shall gather the lambs with his arm, and carry them in his bosom, and . . . gently lead those that are with young" sets us free from those foolish worries that ordinarily trouble us. It is in dedication that we, like Hannah, find a new and triumphant peace.

Since Thou, O God, didst give to us Thine only Son, in perfect love, I gladly dedicate my child to Thee. Work out Thy plan for his life; use him in Thy service. And with this dedication I surrender any anxious thoughts, conscious or subconscious, concerning his health, safety, and future. In the name of Jesus. Amen.

THE HOUSEWIFE

Jesus, teach me how to be
Proud of my simplicity.

Sweep the floors, wash the clothes,
Gather for each vase a rose.

Iron and mend a tiny frock
Taking notice of the clock,

Always having time kept free
For childish questions asked of me.

Grant me wisdom Mary had
When she taught her little Lad.

CATHERINE CATE COBLENTZ

His Physical Care

"And whosoever shall give to drink unto one of these little ones a cup of cold water only in the name of a disciple, Verily I say unto you, he shall in no wise lose his reward."

MATTHEW 10:42

One of the hardest things to understand about our God is how He can on one hand rule the universe in infinite power, and at the same time keep an accurate record of the number of hairs on our head. Since our finite minds cannot grasp such a complex system of eternal bookkeeping, we of little faith find it difficult to believe that we shall be rewarded for so small a service as a cup of cold water given in the name of Jesus.

Have you ever wondered how far around the world a two-year diaper wash would go, if all the diapers you launder in that time were hung on a clothesline side by side? Have you ever been tempted to think that you had nothing to show for your day's work after a day in which the baby took more care than usual, perhaps crying a great deal and making extra laundry? If you have ever felt that all the detailed, intimate, time-consuming duties that go with the physical care of a baby are unnoticed by God, then reread Matthew 10:42.

Helping the newborn infant to satisfy his biological needs, such as sucking, sleeping, feeling the mother's gentle touch, and so on, is an important part of mothering. We are told that the way a mother feeds, washes, or diapers her baby conveys to him her love and concern even before he can understand the meaning of her words. How important, then, it is that we perform these duties in a spirit of love and devotion.

We care for our babies in the name of Christ when we do each little task as unto Him, putting love into everything we do. We do all our daily work in Christ's name when we seek His guidance and blessing, even on the smallest duties of our days.

Heavenly Father, I never realized how many problems a new mother faces until I became a mother myself. I thank Thee for the many helpful books on child care and for kind friends and good doctors who are ready to give a word of encouragement and assistance. As I follow my daily schedule of feeding, bathing, diapering, and comforting my baby, may I seek Thy help in each small task, doing it all with tender care, as unto Thee. Amen.

BABY'S SMILE

The doctors and the nurses state
  My baby's smile's a fake.
It's not a smile at all, they say,
  It's just the tummy ache.

But Grandma's explanation
  Is much nicer, far, than this—
An angel stooped from heaven
  And gave my babe a kiss.

HELEN GOOD BRENNEMAN

His Emotional Care

"That they may teach the young women to be sober,
to love their husbands, to love their children."

TITUS 2:4

"Say, Mamma, let's laugh." With these words one little fellow told his mother that he needed some fun, a bit of her joyous companionship. Perhaps the mother was very busy at the moment and did not sense that her child felt just a little lonely, that he needed her. Is that not the trouble with us mammas? We are sometimes so busy taking care of our children's physical bodies, that we forget their inner need, their emotional care.

Those who study children tell us that pleasant experiences cause children to develop feelings of love and that "bad" children are often "unhappy" children. Insufficient parental affection is bound to show up in a child's personality and behavior, for little children just do not develop as they should, physically, mentally, or spiritually, when their hunger for love is not satisfied.

One doctor, in speaking of a child's need for love, made this statement: "The newly born infant needs to feel mother's bodily contacts, her light caresses; he needs to hear her soft words of delight, and to have prompt attention to his every physical need. At all ages he needs to feel that he is wanted and loved, not so much because of his being good but because he is himself."

Although God has bountifully blessed us with a natural love for our babies, we need to learn to express the love meaningfully to the child. Giving intelligent love takes time, thought, and patience, and like vitamins is a daily requirement. But the confidence our children have in us, and the companionship they share with us, will be well worth all the time and energy we invest in demonstrating to them how much we love them.

O God, Thou art love itself, and Thou hast shed light and love into my soul. Only Thou, dear Father, knowest how the seams of my heart are bursting with affection for this little mite. Help me to remember that life out in this world is very different from the security and warmth of my body, where he lived the first nine months of his existence. Help me to hold him tenderly; help him to understand that he is loved and wanted. Amen.

· 63 ·

THE TEACHER

Lord, who am I to teach the way
  To little children day by day,
  So prone myself to go astray?

I teach them knowledge, but I know
  How faint the flicker and how low
  The candles of my knowledge glow.

I teach them power to will and do,
  But only now to learn anew
  My own great weakness through and through.

I teach them love for all mankind
  And all God's creatures, but I find
  My love comes lagging far behind.

Lord, if their guide I still must be,
  Oh, let the little children see
  The teacher leaning hard on Thee.

LESLIE PINCKNEY HILL

His Intellectual Care

"And thou shalt teach them [God's commandments] diligently unto thy children, and shalt talk of them when thou sittest in thine house, and when thou walkest by the way, and when thou liest down, and when thou risest up."

DEUTERONOMY 6:7

Does a child really learn half of all he will ever know by the time he is three years old, as some people believe? If he does, then H. W. Beecher's statement, "The mother's heart is the child's schoolroom," is a real challenge to mothers.

What kind of intellectual care will our baby get while he is still in our "schoolroom," long before he ever actually goes to school? What courses will we teach him? Will his surrounding classroom (our home) be artistic and teach him the meaning of beauty? Will his playground equipment (his toys) teach him to do constructive things? Will we carefully answer his questions? Will there be good books and good music to develop his early tastes? Most important of all, will the Bible be the chief book in our library?

Most people think that the public school alone educates their children. This is a serious mistake. By the time those curls and pigtails bob into a schoolroom, the children should have completed many courses in Christian living: obedience, respect for parents and teachers, love for others, love for God. They should have had many other classes, too: handicraft, drawing, music, home economics, etc. Daddy as President, Mother as Dean, and both as Instructors should have been educating ever since the babies first began to co-ordinate mind and muscle in the world's greatest school—the home.

Long ago Solomon said, "For as he *thinketh* in his heart, so is he." And Jesus said, "Thou shalt love the Lord thy God with all thy heart, and with all thy soul, and with all thy strength, and with all thy *mind*."

O Lord, I thank Thee for the privilege of playing with my baby, of surrounding him with worth-while toys and books and music, of teaching him the many basic lessons of life. May he learn, as he grows older, that Thou art the source of all beauty, all knowledge, and all wisdom. This I ask in Thy most worthy name. Amen.

· 65 ·

AT FOUR WEEKS

His tiny fists are clenched above his head—
His fair, round face is sweet in infant sleep—
And as I finger fringes of the shawl
That lies so slight and soft against my dress,
I pray for him:
   Lord, may he love this place—
   This house of Thine, erected by Thy grace
   Where Thy dear Word is taught, Thy praises sung.
   Oh, true, he is so very, very young
   And he may cry within these walls, or shout
   In happy, babyish mischief, or call out
   To Daddy in the pulpit. True, he may
   Not understand what Daddy has to say—
   The implications of the Trinity
   Or what "Atonement" means to him and me.
   It may be, first, that folding hands in prayer
   Is all the fellowship his soul can share.
   But as his Saviour grew, oh, may he grow.
   In sure and silent ways, may his heart know
   That Thou art here. And may my conduct be
   A commentary on my love to Thee—
   An explanation louder than my speech
   To reach where Daddy's sermons may not reach.
The singing is resumed; the Scripture's read . . .
The tiny fists now stir above his head.
A little dream-smile flits across his face.
Oh, may he learn to love this holy place!

MIRIAM SIEBER LIND

His Spiritual Care

"Train up a child in the way he should go: and when he
is old, he will not depart from it."   PROVERBS 22:6
     "Bring them up in the nurture and admonition of the
Lord."   EPHESIANS 6:4b

How many times Jesus expressed His love and respect for little
children! On that sacred day in Peter's life when Jesus asked him
three times over if he really loved Him, He charged him first of all to
feed His lambs, and then He told him to feed His sheep. Of every
Christian parent Christ expects spiritual care of the little ones. "Mother, do you really love me? Then feed my lambs."

It matters *what* we feed little lambs. We do not take them out on
the hillside and give them large tufts of stout wire grass. Likewise, a
child understands and digests only those spiritual truths which fit into
his own limited experience. We must know God's Word, know our
children, and then adapt our singing and teaching to the understanding of the child.

How we feed the lambs is also important. One well-meaning
father forced his hungry little boy to learn a verse of Scripture every
morning before breakfast. The boy naturally grew to dislike the Bible.
Unwise parents have been known to use Bible reading as punishment for their children. How could these children grow up to love the
Word of God?

The *when* and *where* of lamb feeding is all the time and everywhere. Robbie Trent, in *Your Child and God*, says, "Shall I teach my
child of God? I am answering that question every day. For good or
for ill, positively or negatively, for faith or for fear, I am teaching my
child of God."

There will be times when we give our lambs direct nurture: Bible
stories, verses, hymns, and prayers, Sunday-school and church experiences. But the indirect nurture of love and faithfulness in all our
ways make the words meaningful when we tell the little ones of their
loving heavenly Father.

*Our Father, we cannot yet teach this tiny child to pray. But help
us, his mother and father, to treat him and each other in such a way
that when he does talk with Thee, he will know that Thou art kind
and good and loving and just and forgiving. Amen.*

· 67 ·

WHERE DID HE GO?

I'll only have this little boy but once.
Sometime, a few years hence,
You'll come to visit, and you'll ask,
"Where did that little tousled-headed,
*   brown-eyed infant go?"*
And I will say,
"I do not really know.
I only know that now a man,
Tall, self-possessed, intelligent,
Is here instead.
But where that scamp'ring little fellow went,
The one who threw my good shoes out the door
And tossed his dinner plate upon the floor
And tore the pages from my best-loved book
And haunted every corner, crevice, nook,
I do not know, I cannot really say
Just where he went, but here to stay
Is this tall lad—
Our little boy in larger garments clad."

HELEN GOOD BRENNEMAN

Sweet childish days, that were as long
*   As twenty days are now.*

W. WORDSWORTH

Watching Him Grow

"And the child grew, and waxed strong in spirit, filled
    with wisdom:
And the grace of God was upon him."   LUKE 2:40

A very little boy I once knew came running in to his mother one
day, laughing heartily at a joke on an older friend of the family.

"He waved at me. He thought I was Daddy."

And that is how it seemed to the little fellow, less than five years
old. To small children the world does not look the same as it does to
older people. That is why they are so often misunderstood.

Each stage of a child's life is different, and wonderful! When
children are still tiny babies, it sometimes seems that they do something new and startling every day. We need to understand the changes
they are making and their special needs at various ages, so that we can
more intelligently help them. There is nothing more thrilling than
watching them grow, but we dare not simply sit back and watch, for
we must guide them in developing their powers to the fullest. We
must direct their energies into constructive and worth-while channels.

The study of child nature will help us to understand and solve
the problems confronting us and our little ones. Reading good books
on child development is a wise investment of time and money for any
parent. Of course, since doctors and research students who study and
write about child growth are not always Christian, we must read their
books with discretion, remembering that our children can never be
really "good" without the help of God.

And what a unique privilege we have, as Christian parents, of
going to God's Word for the basic principles in solving all our problems in life! For we want our children, like the little boy Jesus, not
only to grow and to wax strong in spirit, increasing in wisdom, but to
experience the grace of God upon their lives.

*All-wise Father, we thank Thee for the changes that time brings
upon all of us: for growth of little children, for maturity that comes
with the years. We would not have our children remain babes, either
physically, emotionally, intellectually, or spiritually. As this infant
grows, day by day, into childhood and adulthood help me, his mother,
to guide his feet in the narrow path that leads to life. Amen.*

· 69 ·

A MOTHER'S PRAYER

Father in heaven, make me wise,
  So that my gaze may never meet
A question in my children's eyes.
  God keep me always kind and sweet,

And patient, too, before their need;
  Let each vexation know its place,
Let gentleness be all my creed,
  Let laughter live upon my face!

A mother's day is very long,
  There are so many things to do!
But never let me lose my song
  Before the hardest day is through.

MARGARET E. SANGSTER

Wisdom for Today

"If any of you lack wisdom, let him ask of God, that giveth to all men liberally, and upbraideth not; and it shall be given him. But let him ask in faith, nothing wavering."

"Be not wise in your own conceits."

JAMES 1:5, 6 AND ROMANS 12:16c

Oh, for just a little of the wisdom of Solomon, we cry, looking at the responsibilities placed on our mother shoulders and then at our own weak selves! How can we lead our little ones in straight paths when we ourselves have so many unsolved problems? We can see the mistakes of others, but how can we be sure that we will not make some which are just as bad, or even worse?

But He who said that His strength is made perfect in our weakness can use our very mistakes to show us His better way. Even Solomon himself uttered this prayer: "And now, O Lord my God, thou hast made thy servant king instead of David my father: *and I am but a little child:* I know not how to go out or come in. . . . Give therefore thy servant an understanding heart. . . ."

God honored Solomon's prayer, and in Ephesians 1:17 we are told that we today may be given "the spirit of wisdom and revelation in the knowledge of him." To every believing Christian the Holy Spirit is promised, and He it is who will lead us into all truth.

"I said to the man who stood at the gate of the years,
  'Give me a light that I may find my way.'
But he replied,
  'Go out into the darkness and put your hand in
    the hand of God.
This will be better than light
And safer than a known way.'"

AUTHOR UNKNOWN

My loving heavenly Father, I praise Thee for the way that Thou hast guided my feet until this day, even though I often plod along in the darkness alone, forgetting Thy interest in my life. Gladly do I place my hand in Thine. Humbly do I ask Thy wisdom and Thy strength. Give therefore Thy servant an understanding heart. In Jesus' name. Amen.

WHAT GOD HATH PROMISED

God hath not promised
 Skies always blue,
Flower-strewn pathways
 All our lives through;
God hath not promised
 Sun without rain,
Joy without sorrow,
 Peace without pain.

But God hath promised
 Strength for the day,
Rest for the labor,
 Light for the way,
Grace for the trials,
 Help from above,
Unfailing sympathy,
 Undying love.

ANNIE JOHNSON FLINT

Strength for Today

"I can do all things through Christ which strengtheneth me."

PHILIPPIANS 4:13

"My grace is sufficient for thee:
For my strength is made perfect in weakness."

II CORINTHIANS 12:9a

During the early months following the birth of a new baby, we mothers feel like a friend of mine who crossed the Atlantic in a four-motor plane which was only operating on two motors because of engine trouble. Just as her trip, instead of being quick and pleasant, was long and tedious, so the routine work which we usually enjoy becomes somewhat laborious.

But it is important that we accept this fact as a very small inconvenience for so great a gift, that we remember it is only a temporary experience and common to womankind, and that we do not let our spiritual vim and vigor lag with our physical.

For it is of spiritual strength that the Prophet Isaiah writes:
"He giveth power to the faint; and to them that have no might
    he increaseth strength. . . .
But they that wait upon the Lord shall renew their strength;
    they shall mount up with wings as eagles;
    they shall run, and not be weary;
    and they shall walk, and not faint."

Let us not, however, waste our energies and our strength and then expect God to renew them. If we are to regain our old vitality, we must observe the laws of health: get plenty of rest, the right kind of food, sufficient vitamins. We can serve simple meals, sit down to do some routine chores, lie down with our babies when we nurse them.

God promises strength, as well as material blessings, in one-day doses only. If we wait upon Him and use common sense in the use of our limited energies, we can be assured that He will give "strength for today and bright hope for tomorrow."

O God, I thank Thee for the power which Thou givest to the faint. I know that it will not be long until I once more can run and not be weary, and walk and not faint. Until then, O Father, teach me to be patient. Give me the grace and wisdom to conserve my energies for the most important tasks. In Jesus' name I ask this. Amen.

THE LORD IS MY SHEPHERD

"The Lord is my shepherd;
I shall not want.

He maketh me to lie down in green pastures:
He leadeth me beside the still waters.
He restoreth my soul:
He leadeth me in the paths of righteousness
*   for his name's sake.*

Yea, though I walk through the valley of the shadow of death,
I will fear no evil:
For thou art with me;
Thy rod and thy staff they comfort me.

Thou preparest a table before me
In the presence of mine enemies:
Thou anointest my head with oil;
My cup runneth over.

Surely goodness and mercy shall follow me all the days of my life:
And I will dwell in the house of the Lord for ever."

PSALM 23

Courage for Today

"Be strong and of a good courage;
Be not afraid, neither be thou dismayed:
For the Lord thy God is with thee whithersoever thou goest."

JOSHUA 1:9

Our Task:
"Bring them up in the nurture and admonition of the Lord."

EPHESIANS 6:4b

Our Goal:
"And this is life eternal, that they might know thee the only true God,
and Jesus Christ whom thou hast sent."   JOHN 17:3

Our Resources:
"Wherefore take unto you the whole armour of God . . .
    having your loins girt about with truth,
    and having on the breastplate of righteousness;
    and your feet shod with the preparation of the gospel of peace:
Above all, taking the shield of faith . . .
    and take the helmet of salvation,
    and the sword of the Spirit, which is the word of God."

EPHESIANS 6:13-17

Our God:
". . . and, lo, I am with you alway, even unto the end of the world."

MATTHEW 28:20b

Prayer for Today: Repeat thoughtfully Psalm 23.

Lord, Make Me a Channel of Thy Peace,

That where there is hatred I may bring love,
That where there is wrong I may bring the spirit of forgiveness,
That where there is discord I may bring harmony,
That where there is error I may bring truth,
That where there is doubt I may bring faith,
That where there is despair I may bring hope,
That where there are shadows I may bring light,
That where there is sadness I may bring joy.

Lord, Grant That I May Seek Rather

To comfort than to be comforted,
To understand than to be understood,
To love than to be loved;
                        for
It is by giving that one receives,
It is by self-forgetting that one finds,
It is by dying that one awakens to eternal life.

ST. FRANCIS OF ASSISI

The Rewards of Motherhood

"Who can find a virtuous woman?
For her price is far above rubies."

PROVERBS 31:10

After reading King Solomon's account of the ceaseless activity of the virtuous woman, who "riseth . . . while it is yet night," and of her never-tiring efforts to look well to the ways of her household, someone who does not understand mothers might be tempted to ask what *she* gets out of it all.

Motherhood, however, does not need to seek rewards. There are ample compensations and many daily "surprise packages." As St. Francis prayed, "It is by giving that one receives . . . by self-forgetting that one finds." Solomon describes in detail many of the duties of the Christian wife and mother, but a careful reading shows that she is not a slave to be pitied. Here are a few of her rewards:

The heart of her husband doth safely trust in her.

She is not afraid of the snow for her household.

Her husband is known in the gates.

Her children . . . call her blessed.

Her husband . . . praiseth her.

She shall rejoice in time to come.

Of course, we do not work for praise; indeed, if we look for it we shall not find it. Love seeketh not her own. Nor do we care for flattery.

Like other human beings, mother needs occasionally to be reassured that she is making her loved ones happy. But her children pay her the highest tribute when they love and serve Him who once said of a woman, "She hath done what she could."

Prayer for Today: Read the prayer of St. Francis of Assisi on opposite page.

Acknowledgments

The publisher attempted to trace the ownership of all poems and quotations and to the best of his knowledge has secured all necessary permissions from authors or holders of copyrights. Should there be any oversight in making proper acknowledgment, upon notification of the same the publisher will be pleased to correct such omissions in any future editions of this publication.

For permission to reprint from copyrighted works, the author and publisher are indebted to the sources listed below.

W. W. Coblentz for the poem "The Housewife" by Catherine Cate Coblentz from *Christ and the Fine Arts*, Harper and Brothers (1938).

Macmillan Company for the poem "Everlasting Mercy" from *Poems* by John Masefield, The Macmillan Company.

Cynthia Pearl Maus for the poem "A Mother" Author Unknown from *Christ and the Fine Arts*, Harper and Brothers (1938).

Mabel Niedermeyer McCaw for the poem "I Tried to Lead a Child Through Play."

Moody Press for the passages quoted from *The New Testament*, Tr. Charles B. Williams, Moody Press (1937).

Robbie Trent for a quotation from *Your Child and God* by Robbie Trent, Harper and Brothers (1952).

Charles L. Wallis for the poem "A Mother's Prayer" by Margaret E. Sangster from *Masterpieces of Religious Verse*, Harper and Brothers (1948).

MAD LIBS®

MAD LIBS® is a game for people who don't like games. It can be played by one, two, three, four, or forty.

■ RIDICULOUSLY SIMPLE DIRECTIONS

In this tablet you will find stories containing blank spaces where words are left out. One player, the **READER**, selects one of these stories. The **READER** does not tell anyone what the story is about. Instead he/she asks the other players, the **WRITERS**, to give him/her words. These words are used to fill in the blank spaces in the story.

■ TO PLAY

The **READER** asks each **WRITER** in turn to call out a word. This word will be an adjective or a noun or whatever the space calls for. He/She then writes the words in the blank spaces in the story. After all the spaces are filled in, the result is a **MAD LIB**.

The **READER** then reads the completed **MAD LIB** to the other players. They will hear that they have written a story that is fantastic, screamingly funny, shocking, silly, crazy, or just plain dumb—depending upon which words each **WRITER** called out.

In case you've forgotten what adjectives, adverbs, nouns, and verbs are, here is a quick review:

An **ADJECTIVE** describes something or somebody. *Lumpy, soft, ugly, messy,* and *short* are adjectives.

An **ADVERB** tells how something is done. It modifies a verb and usually ends in "ly." *Modestly, stupidly, greedily,* and *carefully* are adverbs.

A **NOUN** is the name of a person, place, or thing. *Sidewalk, umbrella, bridle, bathtub,* and *nose* are nouns.

A **VERB** is an action word. *Run, pitch, jump,* and *swim* are verbs.

When we ask for a **GEOGRAPHICAL LOCATION**, we mean any sort of place: a country or city (Spain, Cleveland) or a room (bathroom, kitchen).

An **EXCLAMATION** or **SILLY WORD** is any sort of funny sound, gasp, grunt, or outcry. *Wow! Ouch! Whomp! Ick! Gadzooks!* are exclamations and silly words.

When we ask for specific words like **A NUMBER, A COLOR, AN ANIMAL,** or **A PART OF THE BODY,** we mean a word that is one of those things.

When a **PLURAL** is asked for, be sure to pluralize the word. For example, *cat* pluralized is *cats.*

EXAMPLE:
(BEFORE)

"_____!" he said
EXCLAMATION

_____, as he jumped into his
ADVERB

convertible_____and drove off
NOUN

with his _____ wife.
ADJECTIVE

(AFTER)

" *Ouch!* _____!" he said
EXCLAMATION

Stupidly _____, as he jumped into his
ADVERB

convertible_____ *cat* _____and drove off
NOUN

with his _____ *brave* _____ wife.
ADJECTIVE

MAD LIBS® is fun to play with friends, but you can also play it by yourself!
To begin with, DO NOT look at the story on the page below. Fill in the blanks on this page with the words called for. Then, using the words you've selected, fill in the blank spaces in the story. Now you've created your own hilarious MAD LIB!

SPACE SHUTTLE

NOUN: _____

NOUN: _____

ADJECTIVE: _____

PLURAL NOUN: _____

VERB ENDING IN "ING": _____

PLURAL NOUN: _____

A CITY: _____

PLURAL NOUN: _____

NUMBER: _____

SOMETHING ROUND: _____

NUMBER: _____

ADVERB: _____

A PLACE: _____

ADJECTIVE: _____

THE SPACE SHUTTLE

In 1981, the U.S. launched the first real Space _____. It
NOUN

was called a/an _____ Shuttle because it not only went
NOUN

up into _____ space, it also came back. It was named
ADJECTIVE

the "Columbia" and was piloted by two brave _____.
PLURAL NOUN

They had practiced _____ for two years and
VERB ENDING IN "ING"

were expert _____. The Columbia took off from
PLURAL NOUN

_____ using its powerful first stage _____.
A CITY   PLURAL NOUN

At an altitude of _____ feet, it went into orbit around
NUMBER

the _____. After _____ orbits, the
SOMETHING ROUND   NUMBER

Shuttle landed _____ at _____. It was a/an
ADVERB   A PLACE

_____ day for the U.S. Space Program.
ADJECTIVE

From *The Original Mad Libs*® ● Copyright © 1988 Price Stern Sloan, Inc.,

A member of The Putnam & Grosset Group, New York, New York.

MAD LIBS® is fun to play with friends, but you can also play it by yourself!
To begin with, DO NOT look at the story on the page below. Fill in the blanks
on this page with the words called for. Then, using the words you've selected, fill
in the blank spaces in the story.
Now you've created your own hilarious MAD LIB!

NEWSPAPER ARTICLE

ADJECTIVE: _____

ADJECTIVE: _____

ADJECTIVE: _____

NOUN: _____

NOUN: _____

ADVERB: _____

NOUN: _____

NOUN: _____

NOUN: _____

EXCLAMATION: _____

ADJECTIVE: _____

NOUN: _____

NEWSPAPER ARTICLE

Mrs. Fifi Vanderbold, the _____ and _____
              ADJECTIVE   ADJECTIVE

heiress, has filed for divorce from her husband, Percy Vanderbold,

the former _____ _____ of Harvard, class
          ADJECTIVE   NOUN

of '38, now in the _____ business. Mrs. Vanderbold
              NOUN

claimed that her husband had _____ given her a/an
              ADVERB

_____ in the eye and had kicked her twice in the
  NOUN

_____ and the _____. Mr. Vanderbold,
  NOUN   NOUN

when asked to comment, said "_____! This is a/an
                 EXCLAMATION

_____ lie. I only pinched her in the_____."
 ADJECTIVE   NOUN

MAD LIBS® is fun to play with friends, but you can also play it by yourself!
To begin with, DO NOT look at the story on the page below. Fill in the blanks
on this page with the words called for. Then, using the words you've selected, fill
in the blank spaces in the story.
Now you've created your own hilarious MAD LIB!

DESCRIPTION OF THE LOVELY GROUP THAT I AM IN

ADJECTIVE: _____

ADJECTIVE: _____

NAME OF PERSON IN ROOM: _____

ADVERB: _____

PLURAL NOUN: _____

NUMBER: _____

ADJECTIVE: _____

ADVERB: _____

NAME OF PERSON IN ROOM: _____

ADJECTIVE: _____

NOUN: _____

NAME OF PERSON IN ROOM: _____

NOUN: _____

ADJECTIVE: _____

A LIQUID: _____

ADJECTIVE: _____

ADJECTIVE: _____

DESCRIPTION OF THE LOVELY GROUP THAT I AM IN

We are having a perfectly _____ time this evening in the
ADJECTIVE

_____ home of _____. The rooms
ADJECTIVE   NAME OF PERSON IN ROOM

are decorated _____ with many stylish _____
ADVERB   PLURAL NOUN

that must have cost at least _____ dollars. The guests are
NUMBER

all _____ conversationalists and are all _____
ADJECTIVE   ADVERB

dressed. _____ has been entertaining us by
NAME OF PERSON IN ROOM

telling about the time he showed his _____ _____
ADJECTIVE   NOUN

to _____, who mistook it for an early American
NAME OF PERSON IN ROOM

_____. The refreshments are _____ and the
NOUN   ADJECTIVE

idea of serving _____ on the rocks showed _____
A LIQUID   ADJECTIVE

imagination. Visiting here is always a/an _____ exper-
ADJECTIVE

ience.

MAD LIBS® is fun to play with friends, but you can also play it by yourself!
To begin with, DO NOT look at the story on the page below. Fill in the blanks
on this page with the words called for. Then, using the words you've selected, fill
in the blank spaces in the story.
Now you've created your own hilarious MAD LIB!

QUICK QUIZ

ADJECTIVE: _____

NUMBER: _____

GEOGRAPHICAL LOCATION: _____

EXCLAMATION: _____

NUMBER: _____

ADJECTIVE: _____

ADJECTIVE: _____

PLURAL NOUN: _____

ADVERB: _____

ADJECTIVE: _____

PERSON'S NAME: _____

NOUN: _____

PLURAL NOUN: _____

ADJECTIVE: _____

NOUN: _____

NAME OF PERSON IN ROOM: _____

QUICK QUIZ

Who am I? I am a/an _____ American. I was born
                              ADJECTIVE

_____ years ago in _____. When my
      NUMBER   GEOGRAPHICAL LOCATION

father first saw me he said, " _____!" I am
                                    EXCLAMATION

_____ feet tall, have _____ brown eyes, and
      NUMBER   ADJECTIVE

a/an _____ complexion. My hobby is collecting
          ADJECTIVE

_____. I always speak _____ and I have
   PLURAL NOUN   ADVERB

made several _____ motion pictures. I am married to
                  ADJECTIVE

_____, the well known Hollywood _____.
   PERSON'S NAME   NOUN

I have given away thousands of _____ to charity. My
                                    PLURAL NOUN

most prominent physical characteristics are my _____
                                                    ADJECTIVE

nose and my large _____. Who am I?
                        NOUN

ANSWER: I am _____.
              NAME OF PERSON IN ROOM

MAD LIBS® is fun to play with friends, but you can also play it by yourself!
To begin with, DO NOT look at the story on the page below. Fill in the blanks
on this page with the words called for. Then, using the words you've selected, fill
in the blank spaces in the story.
Now you've created your own hilarious MAD LIB!

ADVICE TO PROSPECTIVE PARENTS

ADJECTIVE: _____

ADJECTIVE: _____

NOUN: _____

NOUN: _____

ADJECTIVE: _____

NOUN: _____

ADJECTIVE: _____

A NUMBER: _____

PLURAL NOUN: _____

ADVERB: _____

NOUN: _____

NOUN: _____

PLURAL NOUN: _____

ADVICE TO PROSPECTIVE PARENTS

Congratulations to all of you _____ mothers and
                                    ADJECTIVE

_____ fathers. You are about to give birth to a/an
    ADJECTIVE

_____. Remember, a happy child comes from a happy
      NOUN

_____. Undoubtedly, the _____ will cause
      NOUN   ADJECTIVE

many changes in your life. You'll have to get up at four a.m. to give

the little _____ its bottle of _____
                NOUN   ADJECTIVE

milk. Later, when he's _____ years old, he'll learn
                            A NUMBER

to walk and you'll hear the patter of little _____
                                                PLURAL NOUN

around the house. And in no time he'll be talking _____
                                                        ADVERB

and calling you his "_____" and "_____."
                          NOUN   NOUN

It's no wonder they are called little bundles of _____.
                                                    PLURAL NOUN

MAD LIBS® is fun to play with friends, but you can also play it by yourself!
To begin with, DO NOT look at the story on the page below. Fill in the blanks
on this page with the words called for. Then, using the words you've selected, fill
in the blank spaces in the story.
Now you've created your own hilarious MAD LIB!

HOW TO SERVE WINE

ADVERB: _____

ADJECTIVE: _____

ADJECTIVE: _____

PLURAL NOUN: _____

NOUN: _____

ADJECTIVE: _____

ADJECTIVE: _____

GEOGRAPHICAL LOCATION: _____

PLURAL NOUN: _____

ADJECTIVE: _____

ADJECTIVE: _____

ADJECTIVE: _____

NOUN: _____

PLURAL NOUN: _____

ADVERB: _____

ADJECTIVE: _____

HOW TO SERVE WINE

A good wine, served _____, can make any meal a truly
                          ADVERB

_____ occasion. The red wines have a/an _____
     ADJECTIVE   ADJECTIVE

flavor that blends with boiled _____ or smoked
                                   PLURAL NOUN

_____. White wines range in flavor from _____
       NOUN   ADJECTIVE

to _____. The best wines are made by peasants in
       ADJECTIVE

_____ from the juice of ripe _____,
GEOGRAPHICAL LOCATION   PLURAL NOUN

by putting them in vats and squashing them with their_____
                                                             ADJECTIVE

feet. This is what gives wine that _____ aroma.
                                        ADJECTIVE

Here are a few rules: (1) Always serve white wine in a/an

_____ glass at _____ temperature. (2) Never
     ADJECTIVE   NOUN

serve burgundy with fried _____. (3) Wines should
                              PLURAL NOUN

always be drunk _____ or you're liable to end up with
                     ADVERB

a/an _____ stomach.
         ADJECTIVE

MAD LIBS® is fun to play with friends, but you can also play it by yourself! To begin with, DO NOT look at the story on the page below. Fill in the blanks on this page with the words called for. Then, using the words you've selected, fill in the blank spaces in the story.
Now you've created your own hilarious MAD LIB!

BOOK REVIEW

NAME OF PERSON IN ROOM:_____

NOUN:_____

ADJECTIVE:_____

NOUN:_____

ADJECTIVE:_____

ADJECTIVE:_____

NAME OF GIRL IN ROOM:_____

ADJECTIVE:_____

NONSENSE WORD:_____

NOUN:_____

ADJECTIVE:_____

NOUN:_____

VERB ENDING IN "ING":_____

SAME NAME OF GIRL:_____

ADJECTIVE:_____

ADVERB:_____

A PRESTIGIOUS AWARD:_____

BOOK REVIEW

_____ has just written a book called "The
NAME OF PERSON IN ROOM

_____ in the _____
NOUN   ADJECTIVE

_____." The main character in this
NOUN

_____ story is a/an _____ woman
ADJECTIVE   ADJECTIVE

named _____ who has just been elected president. She
NAME OF GIRL IN ROOM

must decide whether to spend money on making _____
ADJECTIVE

bombs, sending people to the planet _____ or building
NONSENSE WORD

_____ to accomodate the growing population. The au-
NOUN

thor creates many _____ moments and you will find
ADJECTIVE

yourself sitting on the edge of your _____ late at night
NOUN

because you cannot stop _____ this book.
VERB ENDING IN "ING"

_____ turns out to be the greatest president in the last
SAME NAME OF GIRL

century and leads the people to peace and _____. This
ADJECTIVE

book is written _____ and should be nominated for a
ADVERB

_____.
A PRESTIGIOUS AWARD

From _The Original Mad Libs_® ● Copyright © 1988 Price Stern Sloan, Inc.,

A member of The Putnam & Grosset Group, New York, New York.

MAD LIBS® is fun to play with friends, but you can also play it by yourself! To begin with, DO NOT look at the story on the page below. Fill in the blanks on this page with the words called for. Then, using the words you've selected, fill in the blank spaces in the story.
Now you've created your own hilarious MAD LIB!

A STORY WITH A MORAL

NOUN (PLURAL):_____

NOUN (PLURAL):_____

ANIMAL (PLURAL):_____

ADJECTIVE:_____

NOUN (PLURAL):_____

NOUN:_____

VERB (PAST TENSE):_____

NOUN:_____

NONSENSE WORD:_____

NOUN (PLURAL):_____

SAME NONSENSE WORD:_____

SAME ANIMAL (PLURAL):_____

A STORY WITH A MORAL

There once was a very cruel dictator. He would go into foreign

_____ and bring back _____. He taxed
NOUN (PLURAL)   NOUN (PLURAL)

his own people and made them give him _____ as
                                              ANIMAL (PLURAL)

payment for farming the land. Finally, some _____
                                                      ADJECTIVE

young _____ got fed up and organized a protest. They
         NOUN (PLURAL)

fought the oppression by carrying signs that said the dictator was a

_____. After many years of revolt, they finally
        NOUN

_____ the dictator. For punishment, he had to marry a
   VERB (PAST TENSE)

_____ and live in _____ and sew little
        NOUN   NONSENSE WORD

frilly _____ for the rest of his life. The moral of this
          NOUN (PLURAL)

story is: A stitch in _____ saves _____.
                        SAME NONSENSE WORD   SAME ANIMAL (PLURAL)

MAD LIBS® is fun to play with friends, but you can also play it by yourself!
To begin with, DO NOT look at the story on the page below. Fill in the blanks
on this page with the words called for. Then, using the words you've selected, fill
in the blank spaces in the story.
Now you've created your own hilarious MAD LIB!

BEAUTY ADVICE

ADJECTIVE: _____

ADJECTIVE: _____

NOUN: _____

NOUN: _____

A CONTAINER: _____

A LIQUID: _____

A FOOD: _____

A FOOD: _____

ADJECTIVE: _____

ADJECTIVE: _____

NOUN: _____

ADJECTIVE: _____

ADJECTIVE: _____

ADJECTIVE: _____

ADVERB: _____

ADJECTIVE: _____

NAME OF PERSON IN ROOM: _____

BEAUTY ADVICE

If your skin is _____ or _____, you can cure
                    ADJECTIVE   ADJECTIVE

this condition with the following care. Every morning, before

washing your _____, massage it gently with a/an
                     NOUN

_____ that has been soaked overnight in a/an
        NOUN

_____ full of warm _____. Then mix together some
 A CONTAINER   A LIQUID

_____ and some _____ until the mixture
     A FOOD   A FOOD

becomes _____. Pat this onto your _____
              ADJECTIVE   ADJECTIVE

complexion for five minutes. Then remove, using a/an_____,
                                                         NOUN

and wash your face with _____ water. Do not omit this
                              ADJECTIVE

_____ step or your skin will become _____.
     ADJECTIVE   ADJECTIVE

Do this _____ every day and you will soon be as
              ADVERB

_____ as _____.
   ADJECTIVE   NAME OF PERSON IN ROOM

MAD LIBS ™ is fun to play with friends, but you can also play it by yourself!
To begin with, DO NOT look at the story on the page below. Fill in the blanks
on this page with the words called for. Then, using the words you've selected, fill
in the blank spaces in the story.
Now you've created your own hilarious MAD LIB!

NEWSPAPER ADS

ADJECTIVE: _____

ADJECTIVE: _____

ADJECTIVE: _____

ADVERB: _____

ADJECTIVE: _____

NOUN: _____

NOUN: _____

ADJECTIVE: _____

ADJECTIVE: _____

ADJECTIVE: _____

NOUN: _____

NOUN: _____

GEOGRAPHICAL LOCATION: _____

ADJECTIVE: _____

ADJECTIVE: _____

ADJECTIVE: _____

NAME OF PERSON IN ROOM: _____

NOUN: _____

ADJECTIVE: _____

NEWSPAPER ADS

FOR SALE: 1957 Sedan. This _____ car is in a/an
ADJECTIVE

_____ condition. It was formerly owned by a/an
ADJECTIVE

_____ school teacher who always drove it_____.
ADJECTIVE   ADVERB

There is a/an _____ _____ in the back
ADJECTIVE   NOUN

seat and a chrome _____ on the hood. It has a/an
NOUN

_____ paint job, _____ tires, and the back
ADJECTIVE   ADJECTIVE

opens out into a/an _____ _____. Will
ADJECTIVE   NOUN

consider taking slightly used _____ in trade.
NOUN

LOST: In the vicinity of_____, a/an_____
GEOGRAPHICAL LOCATION   ADJECTIVE

French poodle with _____ hair and a/an _____
ADJECTIVE   ADJECTIVE

tail. It answers to the name of_____ and when
NAME OF PERSON IN ROOM

last seen was carrying a/an _____ in its mouth. A/An
NOUN

_____ reward is offered.
ADJECTIVE

MAD LIBS® is fun to play with friends, but you can also play it by yourself! To begin with, DO NOT look at the story on the page below. Fill in the blanks on this page with the words called for. Then, using the words you've selected, fill in the blank spaces in the story.

Now you've created your own hilarious MAD LIB!

FABLE

ADJECTIVE: _____

NOUN: _____

NAME OF PERSON IN ROOM: _____

ADJECTIVE: _____

ADJECTIVE: _____

ADJECTIVE: _____

EXCLAMATION: _____

ADVERB: _____

NOUN: _____

ADJECTIVE: _____

NOUN: _____

ADVERB: _____

ADJECTIVE: _____

ADJECTIVE: _____

NOUN: _____

NOUN: _____

EXCLAMATION: _____

ADJECTIVE: _____

NOUN: _____

NOUN: _____

NOUN: _____

NOUN: _____

NOUN: _____

FABLE

Once upon a time a/an _____ _____
ADJECTIVE   NOUN

expert named _____ felt a/an _____
NAME OF PERSON IN ROOM   ADJECTIVE

pain. He sent for a/an _____ surgeon who looked at his
ADJECTIVE

_____ stomach and said "_____!" Then
ADJECTIVE   EXCLAMATION

he muttered _____, "I see your trouble. The_____
ADVERB   NOUN

on your _____ stomach is overlapping the _____
ADJECTIVE   NOUN

next to your kidney." The surgeon _____ took him to
ADVERB

the _____ operating room of the hospital. There he
ADJECTIVE

made a/an _____ incision reaching from the patient's
ADJECTIVE

_____ to his _____. "_____!"
NOUN   NOUN   EXCLAMATION

said the surgeon. "That takes care of that _____
ADJECTIVE

_____." With that, he began sewing up the incision.
NOUN

However, on the tenth stitch the patient sneezed and almost pulled

the _____ out of the _____, but the surgeon
NOUN   NOUN

took one final stitch and saved the _____. MORAL:
NOUN

A/An _____ in time saves nine.
NOUN

MAD LIBS® is fun to play with friends, but you can also play it by yourself! To begin with, DO NOT look at the story on the page below. Fill in the blanks on this page with the words called for. Then, using the words you've selected, fill in the blank spaces in the story.
Now you've created your own hilarious MAD LIB!

MY DREAM MAN

ADJECTIVE: _____

ADJECTIVE: _____

NAME OF PERSONALITY: _____

NAME OF PERSONALITY: _____

NAME OF ANIMAL: _____

NOUN: _____

NOUN: _____

NOUN: _____

ADVERB: _____

ADJECTIVE: _____

ADVERB: _____

ADJECTIVE: _____

ADJECTIVE: _____

NOUN: _____

ADJECTIVE: _____

NOUN: _____

ADJECTIVE: _____

NAME OF PERSON IN ROOM: _____

MY DREAM MAN

My "Dream Man" should, first of all, be very _____ and
ADJECTIVE

_____. He should have a physique like
ADJECTIVE

_____, a profile like _____,
NAME OF PERSONALITY   NAME OF PERSONALITY

and the intelligence of a/an _____.
NAME OF ANIMAL

He must be polite and always remember to light my _____,
NOUN

to tip his _____, and to take my _____ when
NOUN   NOUN

crossing the street.

He should move _____, should have a/an _____
ADVERB   ADJECTIVE

voice, and should always dress _____. I would also like
ADVERB

him to be a/an _____ dancer, and when we're alone, he
ADJECTIVE

should whisper _____ nothings in my _____
ADJECTIVE   NOUN

and hold my _____ _____.
ADJECTIVE   NOUN

I know a/an _____ man like this is hard to find. In fact,
ADJECTIVE

the only one I can think of is _____.
NAME OF PERSON IN ROOM

From *The Original Mad Libs*® ● Copyright © 1988 Price Stern Sloan, Inc.,
A member of The Putnam & Grosset Group, New York, New York.

MAD LIBS® is fun to play with friends, but you can also play it by yourself! To begin with, DO NOT look at the story on the page below. Fill in the blanks on this page with the words called for. Then, using the words you've selected, fill in the blank spaces in the story.
Now you've created your own hilarious MAD LIB!

HOW TO GO TO SLEEP

ADJECTIVE: _____

ADJECTIVE: _____

A LIQUID: _____

ADJECTIVE: _____

ADJECTIVE: _____

ADVERB: _____

ADJECTIVE: _____

PLURAL NOUN: _____

ADJECTIVE: _____

FEMALE'S NAME: _____

ADJECTIVE: _____

PLURAL NOUN: _____

NOUN: _____

ADJECTIVE: _____

NOUN: _____

HOW TO GO TO SLEEP

If you have trouble falling asleep, you probably have a/an

_____ mind. You must learn to relax so you will have
ADJECTIVE

a/an _____ mind.
ADJECTIVE

First, drink a cup of hot _____ and stretch out on a/an
A LIQUID

_____ bed in a/an _____ position. Then,
ADJECTIVE   ADJECTIVE

breathe _____ and think about something beautiful such
ADVERB

as _____ _____. Do not think about your
ADJECTIVE   PLURAL NOUN

_____ enemies. Concentrate on someone restful, such
ADJECTIVE

as _____, who will make your mind more
FEMALE'S NAME

_____. Or count imaginary _____ jumping
ADJECTIVE   PLURAL NOUN

over a/an _____.
NOUN

Follow these rules and you will fall into a/an _____
ADJECTIVE

sleep the minute your _____ hits the pillow.
NOUN

MAD LIBS® is fun to play with friends, but you can also play it by yourself!
To begin with, DO NOT look at the story on the page below. Fill in the blanks
on this page with the words called for. Then, using the words you've selected, fill
in the blank spaces in the story.
Now you've created your own hilarious MAD LIB!

A FABLE

PLURAL NOUN: _____

ADJECTIVE: _____

NAME OF MAN IN ROOM: _____

ADJECTIVE: _____

NOUN: _____

NOUN: _____

ADJECTIVE: _____

NOUN: _____

NOUN: _____

ADJECTIVE: _____

ADJECTIVE: _____

ADVERB: _____

NOUN: _____

PLURAL NOUN: _____

NOUN: _____

ADJECTIVE: _____

NOUN: _____

NOUN: _____

A FABLE

Once upon a time there was a very curious girl who was always

poking her nose into everybody's _____. She kept
                                                       PLURAL NOUN

company with a/an _____ man named
                                     ADJECTIVE

_____, who was always buying her
            NAME OF MAN IN ROOM

_____ presents. Once he gave her a diamond _____
ADJECTIVE   NOUN

to wear on her _____, and he bought her a/an _____
             NOUN   ADJECTIVE

_____ to wear in her _____. Then one day
       NOUN   NOUN

he bought her a/an _____ horse. As soon as she saw the
                       ADJECTIVE

_____ animal she began to examine it _____.
   ADJECTIVE   ADVERB

First she looked at the horse's _____, and then at its
                                 NOUN

_____. Then she opened its mouth so she could look at
  PLURAL NOUN

its _____. At this, the horse became _____
    NOUN   ADJECTIVE

and bit off her _____.
               NOUN

MORAL: Never look a gift horse in the _____.
                                              NOUN

From *The Original Mad Libs*® ● Copyright © 1988 Price Stern Sloan, Inc.,

A member of The Putnam & Grosset Group, New York, New York.

MAD LIBS® is fun to play with friends, but you can also play it by yourself!
To begin with, DO NOT look at the story on the page below. Fill in the blanks
on this page with the words called for. Then, using the words you've selected, fill
in the blank spaces in the story.
Now you've created your own hilarious MAD LIB!

ARMY INFORMATION

ADJECTIVE: _____

ADJECTIVE: _____

PLURAL NOUN: _____

PLURAL NOUN: _____

NOUN: _____

NOUN: _____

ADVERB: _____

ADJECTIVE: _____

PLURAL NOUN: _____

NOUN: _____

PLURAL NOUN: _____

ADJECTIVE: _____

EXCLAMATION: _____

NOUN: _____

NOUN: _____

ADJECTIVE: _____

NOUN: _____

ARMY INFORMATION

If you plan on joining the army, here are some _____
ADJECTIVE

hints that will help you become a/an _____ soldier. The
ADJECTIVE

army is made up of officers, non-coms, and _____. You
PLURAL NOUN

can recognize an officer by the _____ on his shoulders
PLURAL NOUN

and the _____ on his cap. When you address an officer,
NOUN

always say "_____" and salute _____. If
NOUN   ADVERB

you get a/an _____ hair-cut, keep your_____
ADJECTIVE   PLURAL NOUN

shined, and see that your_____ is clean at all times, you
NOUN

will be a credit to the slogan, "The Army builds _____."
PLURAL NOUN

And at roll call, when the _____ sergeant calls your
ADJECTIVE

name, shout "_____!" loud and clear. Also, become
EXCLAMATION

familiar with basic weapons such as the thirty-calibre _____
NOUN

and the automatic _____. Follow this advice and in no
NOUN

time you'll win the _____ Conduct _____.
ADJECTIVE   NOUN

From *The Original Mad Libs*® ● Copyright © 1988 Price Stern Sloan, Inc.,

A member of The Putnam & Grosset Group, New York, New York.

MAD LIBS® is fun to play with friends, but you can also play it by yourself!
To begin with, DO NOT look at the story on the page below. Fill in the blanks
on this page with the words called for. Then, using the words you've selected, fill
in the blank spaces in the story.
Now you've created your own hilarious MAD LIB!

TRAVEL SUGGESTION

ADJECTIVE: _____

ADJECTIVE: _____

ADJECTIVE: _____

ADJECTIVE: _____

PLURAL NOUN: _____

PLURAL NOUN: _____

ADJECTIVE: _____

NOUN: _____

PLURAL NOUN: _____

NOUN: _____

NOUN: _____

ADJECTIVE: _____

ADJECTIVE: _____

ADJECTIVE: _____

ADJECTIVE: _____

ADJECTIVE: _____

NOUN: _____

ADJECTIVE: _____

TRAVEL SUGGESTION

If you're looking for a place to spend a/an _____
                                              ADJECTIVE

honeymoon, think of _____ Mexico. There, under a
                          ADJECTIVE

brilliant, _____ sky, you and your _____
                ADJECTIVE   ADJECTIVE

bride can spend hours inspecting the quaint_____
                                                  PLURAL NOUN

and the ancient Aztec_____. You will be fascinated
                          PLURAL NOUN

by the_____ customs of the natives. In the evening,
          ADJECTIVE

you can retire to the local _____ which is what the
                                  NOUN

Mexicans call their _____, and watch the famous
                          PLURAL NOUN

_____ dance called the _____.
      NOUN   NOUN

Hotels there have all_____ conveniences, including
                          ADJECTIVE

_____ water, _____ air-conditioning, and
    ADJECTIVE   ADJECTIVE

_____ service. The rates are also very_____.
    ADJECTIVE   ADJECTIVE

In a few days, you and your bride will be lolling on the_____,
                                                            NOUN

just like the _____ natives.
                 ADJECTIVE

MAD LIBS® is fun to play with friends, but you can also play it by yourself! To begin with, **DO NOT** look at the story on the page below. Fill in the blanks on this page with the words called for. Then, using the words you've selected, fill in the blank spaces in the story.
Now you've created your own hilarious MAD LIB!

DESCRIPTION OF WEDDING

ADJECTIVE: _____

ADJECTIVE: _____

NAME OF WOMAN: _____

NAME OF MAN: _____

ADVERB: _____

ADJECTIVE: _____

NOUN: _____

ADJECTIVE: _____

ADJECTIVE: _____

ADJECTIVE: _____

NOUN: _____

ADJECTIVE: _____

NOUN: _____

ADJECTIVE: _____

ADJECTIVE: _____

ADJECTIVE: _____

ADJECTIVE: _____

PLURAL NOUN: _____

GEOGRAPHICAL LOCATION: _____

ADVERB: _____ ____

DESCRIPTION OF WEDDING

The _____ wedding yesterday afternoon between
       ADJECTIVE

_____ _____ and her groom,
  ADJECTIVE   NAME OF WOMAN

_____, was carried off _____. The bride
  NAME OF MAN   ADVERB

wore a long _____ _____ with
      ADJECTIVE   NOUN

_____ edging and a/an _____ neckline. At
  ADJECTIVE   ADJECTIVE

the end of the _____ ceremony, there wasn't a dry
      ADJECTIVE

_____ in the place. Later, at the reception, the bride's
  NOUN

mother said, "The groom is a/an _____ man, just the
        ADJECTIVE

type of _____ we wanted for our _____
    NOUN   ADJECTIVE

daughter." The _____ couple left midst a flurry of
      ADJECTIVE

_____ congratulations, to spend a/an _____
  ADJECTIVE   ADJECTIVE

honeymoon visiting _____ in _____.
      PLURAL NOUN   GEOGRAPHICAL LOCATION

They are sure to live _____ for many years.
        ADVERB

MAD LIBS® is fun to play with friends, but you can also play it by yourself!
To begin with, DO NOT look at the story on the page below. Fill in the blanks
on this page with the words called for. Then, using the words you've selected, fill
in the blank spaces in the story.
Now you've created your own hilarious MAD LIB!

MY DREAM GIRL

ADJECTIVE: _____

PLURAL NOUN: _____

ADJECTIVE: _____

A LIQUID: _____

ADJECTIVE: _____

PLURAL NOUN: _____

ADJECTIVE: _____

NOUN: _____

NAME OF PERSON IN ROOM: _____

EXCLAMATION: _____

ADJECTIVE: _____

ADJECTIVE: _____

ADJECTIVE: _____

ADJECTIVE: _____

NOUN: _____

PLURAL NOUN: _____

ADJECTIVE: _____

NAME OF PERSON IN ROOM: _____

MY DREAM GIRL

The girl of my dreams has _____ blonde hair scented
ADJECTIVE

like _____. Her eyes are like two _____
PLURAL NOUN   ADJECTIVE

pools of _____. And her lips remind me of _____
A LIQUID   ADJECTIVE

_____. Her skin is as smooth and lovely as a/an
PLURAL NOUN

_____ _____, and she has a figure like
ADJECTIVE   NOUN

_____. When she enters a room, people always
NAME OF PERSON IN ROOM

stare at her and say, "_____! What a/an _____
EXCLAMATION   ADJECTIVE

woman!" Her sense of humor is always _____, and
ADJECTIVE

people marvel at her _____ vocabulary. In my dreams I
ADJECTIVE

see her wearing a/an _____ dress and a diamond
ADJECTIVE

_____ in her hair. I would gladly give up all my
NOUN

_____ for one evening with this _____
PLURAL NOUN   ADJECTIVE

female. Her name is _____.
NAME OF PERSON IN ROOM

MAD LIBS® is fun to play with friends, but you can also play it by yourself!
To begin with, DO NOT look at the story on the page below. Fill in the blanks
on this page with the words called for. Then, using the words you've selected, fill
in the blank spaces in the story.
Now you've created your own hilarious MAD LIB!

FABLE

ADJECTIVE: _____

ADJECTIVE: _____

ADJECTIVE: _____

ADJECTIVE: _____

EXCLAMATION: _____

ADJECTIVE: _____

ADJECTIVE: _____

ADJECTIVE: _____

ADJECTIVE: _____

ADJECTIVE: _____

ADVERB: _____

NOUN: _____

NOUN: _____

NOUN: _____

FABLE

Once upon a time a/an _____ dog got hold of a/an
                        ADJECTIVE

_____ bone. He was walking across a/an _____
     ADJECTIVE   ADJECTIVE

bridge and saw his _____ reflection in the water.
                          ADJECTIVE

"_____!" he said. "There is another _____
     EXCLAMATION   ADJECTIVE

dog with another _____ bone. I'll make a/an
                        ADJECTIVE

_____ grab, take his, and then I'll have two _____
     ADJECTIVE   ADJECTIVE

bones." With that the _____ dog jumped into the water
                             ADJECTIVE

and _____ drowned.
          ADVERB

MORAL: A/An _____ in the _____ is
                   NOUN   NOUN

worth two in the _____.
                        NOUN

MAD LIBS® is fun to play with friends, but you can also play it by yourself! To begin with, DO NOT look at the story on the page below. Fill in the blanks on this page with the words called for. Then, using the words you've selected, fill in the blank spaces in the story.

Now you've created your own hilarious MAD LIB!

PROPER CARE OF THE SCALP

ADJECTIVE: _____

ADJECTIVE: _____

ADJECTIVE: _____

ADJECTIVE: _____

NOUN: _____

PLURAL NOUN: _____

ADVERB: _____

ADJECTIVE: _____

NOUN: _____

NOUN: _____

NOUN: _____

ADJECTIVE: _____

NOUN: _____

NOUN: _____

PROPER CARE OF THE SCALP

Don't neglect your scalp! Even though you don't know it, your scalp

may be _____. This can cause your hair to turn
           ADJECTIVE

_____ and _____. A/An _____
  ADJECTIVE   ADJECTIVE   ADJECTIVE

scalp is due to overactivity on the part of the _____
                        NOUN

gland and to excessive production of the _____ normally
                  PLURAL NOUN

present in the skin. For a healthy scalp, wash your head_____
                        ADVERB

every night in _____ water and then take a hot_____
         ADJECTIVE   NOUN

shampoo. Then massage your _____ for five minutes
                NOUN

with a sharp _____. If you suffer from _____
        NOUN   ADJECTIVE

hair, soak your _____ regularly in a/an _____
       NOUN   NOUN

of vinegar. Good luck!

MAD LIBS® is fun to play with friends, but you can also play it by yourself! To begin with, DO NOT look at the story on the page below. Fill in the blanks on this page with the words called for. Then, using the words you've selected, fill in the blank spaces in the story.
Now you've created your own hilarious MAD LIB!

A (SECRET) LETTER FROM AN ADMIRER

NAME OF WOMAN IN ROOM: _____

NOUN: _____

ADJECTIVE: _____

ADJECTIVE: _____

NAME OF PERSON IN ROOM: _____

ADJECTIVE: _____

ADJECTIVE: _____

PLURAL NOUN: _____

ADJECTIVE: _____

ADJECTIVE: _____

ADJECTIVE: _____

ADJECTIVE: _____

ADJECTIVE: _____

ADJECTIVE: _____

ADJECTIVE: _____

ADJECTIVE: _____

ADJECTIVE: _____

NOUN: _____

ADVERB: _____

NAME OF MAN IN ROOM: _____

A (SECRET) LETTER FROM AN ADMIRER

Dear Miss _____,
      NAME OF WOMAN IN ROOM

You may not recall my _____, but I met you at the
                         NOUN

_____ cocktail party given by our _____
   ADJECTIVE   ADJECTIVE

friend, _____. We had a/an _____
         NAME OF PERSON IN ROOM   ADJECTIVE

talk about _____ _____, and I was im-
              ADJECTIVE   PLURAL NOUN

pressed by your _____ conversation and your grasp of
                   ADJECTIVE

the _____ situation. Also, I was very much attracted by
       ADJECTIVE

your_____ eyes, your_____ little chin, and
       ADJECTIVE   ADJECTIVE

your _____ teeth. If you'll pardon me for seeming
        ADJECTIVE

_____, I was fascinated by your_____ walk
   ADJECTIVE   ADJECTIVE

and by your _____ figure.
               ADJECTIVE

I hope I made a/an _____ impression, and that we can
                      ADJECTIVE

get together for a nice _____ next week.
                           NOUN

                          _____ yours,
                              ADVERB

                          _____
                          NAME OF MAN IN ROOM

MAD LIBS® is fun to play with friends, but you can also play it by yourself!
To begin with, DO NOT look at the story on the page below. Fill in the blanks on this page with the words called for. Then, using the words you've selected, fill in the blank spaces in the story. Now you've created your own hilarious MAD LIB!

DRIVING TIPS

ADJECTIVE: _____

NOUN: _____

NOUN: _____

ADJECTIVE: _____

NOUN: _____

NOUN: _____

NOUN: _____

ADJECTIVE: _____

PLURAL NOUN: _____

ADVERB: _____

NOUN: _____

DRIVING TIPS

Driving a car can be fun if you follow this _____ advice:
                                                    ADJECTIVE

1. When approaching a/an _____ on the right, always
                              NOUN

   blow your _____.
                  NOUN

2. Before making a/an _____ turn,
                              ADJECTIVE

   always stick your _____ out of the window.
                          NOUN

3. Every 2000 miles have your _____ inspected
                                    NOUN

   and your _____ checked.
                  NOUN

4. When approaching a school, watch out for _____
                                                  ADJECTIVE

   _____.
       PLURAL NOUN

5. Above all, drive _____. The _____
                          ADVERB   NOUN

   you save may be your own!

MAD LIBS® is fun to play with friends, but you can also play it by yourself! To begin with, DO NOT look at the story on the page below. Fill in the blanks on this page with the words called for. Then, using the words you've selected, fill in the blank spaces in the story.
Now you've created your own hilarious MAD LIB!

PAGE FROM AN ANALYST'S NOTEBOOK

NAME OF FELLOW IN ROOM:_____

NOUN:_____

PLURAL NOUN:_____

ADJECTIVE:_____

ADJECTIVE:_____

VERB:_____

PLURAL NOUN:_____

NOUN:_____

NUMBER:_____

AN ANIMAL:_____

VERB (PRESENT TENSE):_____

NOUN:_____

A SPORT:_____

AN ANIMAL:_____

PAGE FROM AN ANALYST'S NOTEBOOK

This is the case history of _____ who is suffering
NAME OF FELLOW IN ROOM

from a/an _____ complex. He also has abormal fears of
NOUN

_____ and _____ schizophrenia. As a
PLURAL NOUN   ADJECTIVE

child, he had a/an _____ mother who never
ADJECTIVE

let him _____ outside and paid no attention to his
VERB

_____. Also, his father refused to let him play little
PLURAL NOUN

league _____.
NOUN

When he was _____ years old, his _____
NUMBER   AN ANIMAL

ran away on a rainy night which is why he _____
VERB (PRESENT TENSE)

at the moon during thunderstorms.

It's no wonder that today he never leaves the _____,
NOUN

spends all his time watching _____ on TV while
A SPORT

eating boxes of _____ biscuits.
AN ANIMAL

MAD LIBS® is fun to play with friends, but you can also play it by yourself! To begin with, DO NOT look at the story on the page below. Fill in the blanks on this page with the words called for. Then, using the words you've selected, fill in the blank spaces in the story.
Now you've created your own hilarious MAD LIB!

A LETTER FROM CAMP

ADJECTIVE: _____

NOUN: _____

ADJECTIVE: _____

NUMBER: _____

PLURAL NOUN: _____

NOUN: _____

PLURAL NOUN: _____

NAME OF MAN IN ROOM: _____

ADJECTIVE: _____

PLURAL NOUN: _____

PLURAL NOUN: _____

GEOGRAPHICAL LOCATION: _____

NOUN: _____

NOUN: _____

ADJECTIVE: _____

PLURAL NOUN: _____

ADJECTIVE: _____

NAME OF MAN IN ROOM: _____

A LETTER FROM CAMP

Dear Mommy and Daddy,

This camp you sent me to is _____. We go
                                    ADJECTIVE

_____-back riding every day. I am in a/an _____
       NOUN   ADJECTIVE

tent with _____ other _____. After dark we
                NUMBER   PLURAL NOUN

play _____ until our counselor comes around and turns
           NOUN

off our _____. Our counselor is named
                  PLURAL NOUN

_____ and he shows us how to make
    NAME OF MAN IN ROOM

_____ _____ out of used _____.
   ADJECTIVE   PLURAL NOUN   PLURAL NOUN

Tomorrow we are going on a hike through _____
                                          GEOGRAPHICAL LOCATION

and our counselor says whoever brings back the biggest _____
                                                          NOUN

will get an extra _____ for dinner. Please send me some
                       NOUN

_____ underwear and two pairs of _____.
   ADJECTIVE   PLURAL NOUN

Your _____ son, _____
        ADJECTIVE   NAME OF MAN IN ROOM

MAD LIBS® is fun to play with friends, but you can also play it by yourself! To begin with, DO NOT look at the story on the page below. Fill in the blanks on this page with the words called for. Then, using the words you've selected, fill in the blank spaces in the story.

Now you've created your own hilarious MAD LIB!

MY MOST EMBARRASSING MOMENT

NAME OF GIRL IN ROOM: _____

ADJECTIVE: _____

GEOGRAPHICAL LOCATION: _____

ADJECTIVE: _____

NOUN: _____

NOUN: _____

NOUN: _____

NOUN: _____

NOUN: _____

PLURAL NOUN: _____

ADJECTIVE: _____

NOUN: _____

ADJECTIVE: _____

NOUN: _____

NOUN: _____

MY MOST EMBARRASSING MOMENT

By _____
       NAME OF GIRL IN ROOM

My embarrassing moment happened when I got on a/an _____
                                                      ADJECTIVE

bus to go to _____. The bus was very
             GEOGRAPHICAL LOCATION

_____, so I stood up and held on to a/an _____.
  ADJECTIVE   NOUN

At the next stop I saw a/an _____ get up and I ran over to
                              NOUN

grab his _____, but I accidentally jabbed my
            NOUN

_____ into his _____ and broke his
   NOUN   NOUN

_____. And then as I was apologizing, the bus came to
 PLURAL NOUN

a/an _____ stop, which caused me to drop my
       ADJECTIVE

_____ and fall on top of a/an _____ lady
   NOUN   ADJECTIVE

who was carrying a/an _____ on her lap. Believe me, my
                         NOUN

_____ was red that day!
   NOUN

MAD LIBS® is fun to play with friends, but you can also play it by yourself!
To begin with, DO NOT look at the story on the page below. Fill in the blanks
on this page with the words called for. Then, using the words you've selected, fill
in the blank spaces in the story.
Now you've created your own hilarious MAD LIB!

SAVING GASOLINE

A PLACE: _____

ADJECTIVE: _____

PLURAL NOUN: _____

ADJECTIVE: _____

PLURAL NOUN: _____

NOUN: _____

ADJECTIVE: _____

A SILLY WORD: _____

A LIQUID: _____

PLURAL NOUN: _____

ADJECTIVE: _____

NUMBER: _____

NOUN: _____

SAVING GASOLINE

Now that Saudi Arabia and _____ and those other
                            A PLACE

_____ Arab countries have raised the price of gasoline,
   ADJECTIVE

millions of patriotic _____ are trying to economize.
                        PLURAL NOUN

Americans are riding bicycles and _____ small cars.
                                      ADJECTIVE

Many people have turned in their old, gas-guzzling_____
                                                      PLURAL NOUN

and ride to work every day in a/an _____. Scientists are
                                       NOUN

working on _____ substitutes for gas. One is called
              ADJECTIVE

_____. It is made by mixing regular gasoline
   A SILLY WORD

with _____. Other people are depending on electric
        A LIQUID

_____. These are very _____. But there is a
   PLURAL NOUN   ADJECTIVE

problem. You have to stop every _____ miles to have
                                    NUMBER

your _____ recharged!
        NOUN

MAD LIBS® is fun to play with friends, but you can also play it by yourself! To begin with, DO NOT look at the story on the page below. Fill in the blanks on this page with the words called for. Then, using the words you've selected, fill in the blank spaces in the story.

Now you've created your own hilarious MAD LIB!

MAD LIB RECORD OFFER

PLURAL NOUN: _____

NOUN: _____

ADJECTIVE: _____

PLURAL NOUN: _____

ADJECTIVE: _____

NAME OF PERSON IN ROOM: _____

NUMBER: _____

NOUN: _____

NOUN: _____

VERB ENDING IN "ING": _____

NOUN: _____

NOUN: _____

NAME OF MALE IN ROOM: _____

ADJECTIVE: _____

ADJECTIVE: _____

MAD LIB RECORD OFFER

Ladies and _____ of the TV audience, before we return
                 PLURAL NOUN

to our late, late _____ I want to tell you about a/an
                        NOUN

_____ musical offer. For only five dollars and ninety-
      ADJECTIVE

five _____ you can now get all of the _____
      PLURAL NOUN   ADJECTIVE

hits that _____ has put out over the past
               NAME OF PERSON IN ROOM

_____ years. This album is on a four-track _____
      NUMBER   NOUN

and features such hits as "Raindrops Are Falling On My _____"
                                                                    NOUN

and "_____ May Be Dangerous to Your
            VERB ENDING IN "ING"

_____." The album was recorded at the famous Santa
      NOUN

Barbara _____ Festival by the _____
                NOUN   NAME OF MALE IN ROOM

Rock Band featuring the super-_____ guitars. Act now!
                                       ADJECTIVE

This may be your last chance to get such a/an _____
                                                            ADJECTIVE

bargain.

MAD LIBS® is fun to play with friends, but you can also play it by yourself! To begin with, DO NOT look at the story on the page below. Fill in the blanks on this page with the words called for. Then, using the words you've selected, fill in the blank spaces in the story.
Now you've created your own hilarious MAD LIB!

LOVE SCENE

NAME OF GIRL IN ROOM:_____

NAME OF BOY IN ROOM:_____

ADJECTIVE:_____

ADJECTIVE:_____

PLURAL NOUN:_____

NOUN:_____

ADJECTIVE:_____

NOUN:_____

NOUN:_____

VERB ENDING IN "ING":_____

NOUN:_____

NOUN:_____

NOUN:_____

NAME OF CELEBRITY:_____

LOVE SCENE

To be performed by _____ and _____.
             NAME OF GIRL IN ROOM   NAME OF BOY IN ROOM

GIRL: Before I go inside, I want to thank you for a/an _____
                                                        ADJECTIVE

evening. I've really had a/an _____ time.
                                 ADJECTIVE

BOY: I'll bet you tell that to all the _____.
                                          PLURAL NOUN

GIRL: You'd better go now before my _____ hears you
                                        NOUN

and wakes up. He's a very _____ sleeper.
                              ADJECTIVE

BOY: I don't care. Darling, I love you more than _____
                                                     NOUN

itself. Let me take you away from this terrible _____.
                                                   NOUN

GIRL: You've got to be _____. I wouldn't run away
                       VERB ENDING IN "ING"

with you if you were the last _____ on
                                 NOUN

earth.

BOY: But darling, you're breaking my _____. I love
                                        NOUN

you. Please marry me and be my _____.
                                  NOUN

GIRL: I'm sorry, but I'm already engaged to _____.
                                          NAME OF CELEBRITY

MAD LIBS® is fun to play with friends, but you can also play it by yourself! To begin with, DO NOT look at the story on the page below. Fill in the blanks on this page with the words called for. Then, using the words you've selected, fill in the blank spaces in the story.
Now you've created your own hilarious MAD LIB!

A PAGE FROM A GIRL'S DIARY

ADJECTIVE:_____

NAME OF GIRL IN ROOM:_____

ADJECTIVE:_____

NOUN:_____

PLURAL NOUN:_____

NOUN:_____

NOUN:_____

NOUN:_____

VERB ENDING IN "ING":_____

ADJECTIVE:_____

NOUN:_____

ADJECTIVE:_____

NOUN:_____

NAME OF BOY IN ROOM:_____

ADJECTIVE:_____

NOUN:_____

A PAGE FROM A GIRL'S DIARY

This is a/an _____ entry in _____'s
ADJECTIVE   NAME OF GIRL IN ROOM

diary.

Dear Diary: Today I saw him again. When he looks at me with those

_____ eyes, it makes my _____ go pitter-
ADJECTIVE   NOUN

pat, and I feel as if I have _____ in my stomach. I think he
PLURAL NOUN

likes me because he asked me for the _____ when I
NOUN

was standing next to him in the _____. I just had to hear
NOUN

his _____ again, so I callled his _____
NOUN   VERB ENDING IN "ING"

machine and left a _____ message. I hope he doesn't
ADJECTIVE

recognize my _____. He is such a/an _____
NOUN   ADJECTIVE

_____, dear Diary. His name is _____,
NOUN   NAME OF BOY IN ROOM

and I live in hope that someday he will realize how _____ I
ADJECTIVE

would be for him, and that I am the _____ he has
NOUN

always been looking for.

MAD LIBS® is fun to play with friends, but you can also play it by yourself!
To begin with, DO NOT look at the story on the page below. Fill in the blanks
on this page with the words called for. Then, using the words you've selected, fill
in the blank spaces in the story.
Now you've created your own hilarious MAD LIB!

CLUB MEETING

ADJECTIVE: _____

NOUN: _____

NAME OF HOST OR HOSTESS: _____

ADJECTIVE: _____

NAME OF WOMAN IN ROOM: _____

PLURAL NOUN: _____

NAME OF MAN IN ROOM: _____

NOUN: _____

A CELEBRITY: _____

NOUN: _____

NOUN: _____

NAME OF WOMAN IN ROOM: _____

NOUN: _____

ADJECTIVE: _____

NOUN: _____

ADJECTIVE: _____

CLUB MEETING

It's a pleasure to see so many _____ members of our
ADJECTIVE

_____ Club here this evening. I would like to thank
NOUN

_____ for allowing us to meet here in this
NAME OF HOST OR HOSTESS

_____ home. At our last meeting, you will remember,
ADJECTIVE

_____ spoke to us about her experiences
NAME OF WOMAN IN ROOM

among the _____ of Central Mexico. This evening
PLURAL NOUN

_____ has promised to play a few selections on
NAME OF MAN IN ROOM

his _____. And _____ will show us
NOUN A CELEBRITY

how he converted an old _____ into a beautiful
NOUN

_____. Later, _____ will show us
NOUN NAME OF WOMAN IN ROOM

her new _____ and tell us where we can get the materials
NOUN

to make one. Afterwards we will retire to the _____
ADJECTIVE

_____ for some _____ refreshments.
NOUN ADJECTIVE

MAD LIBS® is fun to play with friends, but you can also play it by yourself!
To begin with, DO NOT look at the story on the page below. Fill in the blanks
on this page with the words called for. Then, using the words you've selected, fill
in the blank spaces in the story.
Now you've created your own hilarious MAD LIB!

DRAMATIC SCENE ENTITLED

"THE HAPPY MOMENT"

ADJECTIVE: _____

NOUN: _____

NOUN: _____

LOUD EXCLAMATION: _____

ADJECTIVE: _____

NOUN: _____

PLURAL NOUN: _____

ADJECTIVE: _____

NOUN: _____

A LIQUID: _____

NOUN: _____

NOUN: _____

NOUN: _____

A NUMBER: _____

NOUN: _____

DRAMATIC SCENE ENTITLED
"THE HAPPY MOMENT"

To be played by two brave volunteer actors

WOMAN: Darling, I have something _____ to tell
       ADJECTIVE
you.

MAN: Did you wreck the _____ again?
                          NOUN

WOMAN: No. I went to the doctor's. He says I am going to have a

little _____.
       NOUN

MAN: _____! Sweetheart, that's _____
       LOUD EXCLAMATION   ADJECTIVE

news. Here, sit down here on this _____.
                                   NOUN

You must take the weight off your _____.
                                   PLURAL NOUN

WOMAN: He said I was in _____ health. He measured
                        ADJECTIVE

my _____ and took a sample of my _____.
   NOUN   A LIQUID

MAN: Gee, I wonder if it'll be a boy or a/an _____.
                                                NOUN

WOMAN: Personally, I hope it'll be a/an _____. Then
                                         NOUN

we can name it after your _____.
                           NOUN

MAN: I can hardly believe it. Just think, in _____
                                                A NUMBER
months I'll be a/an _____.
                     NOUN

From *Son of Mad Libs*® ● Copyright © 1988 Price Stern Sloan, Inc.,
A member of The Putnam & Grosset Group. New York. New York.

MAD LIBS® is fun to play with friends, but you can also play it by yourself! To begin with, DO NOT look at the story on the page below. Fill in the blanks on this page with the words called for. Then, using the words you've selected, fill in the blank spaces in the story.

Now you've created your own hilarious MAD LIB!

CHARITY DRIVE LETTER

NAME OF PERSON IN ROOM: _____

ADJECTIVE: _____

PLURAL NOUN: _____

NUMBER: _____

NOUN: _____

PLURAL NOUN: _____

PLURAL NOUN: _____

ADJECTIVE: _____

A CELEBRITY: _____

A CELEBRITY: _____

ADJECTIVE: _____

NOUN: _____

NOUN: _____

ADJECTIVE: _____

A LIQUID: _____

PLURAL NOUN: _____

ADJECTIVE: _____

NOUN: _____

PLURAL NOUN: _____

NAME OF ANOTHER PERSON IN ROOM: _____

CHARITY DRIVE LETTER

Dear _____,
NAME OF PERSON IN ROOM

   I'm sure you've heard of our organization, "The Society for the

Prevention of _____ _____." We are cur-
ADJECTIVE   PLURAL NOUN

rently having a drive to raise _____ dollars to build an
NUMBER

up-to-date _____ for underprivileged _____.
NOUN   PLURAL NOUN

I know that as one of the leading _____ of your
PLURAL NOUN

community you will want to contribute to this _____
ADJECTIVE

cause. Our president _____ and our treasurer
A CELEBRITY

_____ have been connected with many _____
A CELEBRITY   ADJECTIVE

charities. They urge you to reach down into your _____
NOUN

and give. Even if it's only a/an _____. The money will
NOUN

finance our _____ out-patient clinic where anyone who
ADJECTIVE

thinks he has _____ in his _____ can come
A LIQUID   PLURAL NOUN

and have our _____ doctors x-ray his _____.
ADJECTIVE   NOUN

Eventually we hope to stamp out _____ altogether.
PLURAL NOUN

(Signed) _____
NAME OF ANOTHER PERSON IN ROOM

From *Son of Mad Libs*® ● Copyright © 1988 Price Stern Sloan, Inc.,

A member of The Putnam & Grosset Group, New York, New York.

MAD LIBS® is fun to play with friends, but you can also play it by yourself! To begin with, DO NOT look at the story on the page below. Fill in the blanks on this page with the words called for. Then, using the words you've selected, fill in the blank spaces in the story.

Now you've created your own hilarious MAD LIB!

AN ADULT WESTERN

LAST NAME OF MAN IN ROOM: _____

ADVERB: _____

ADJECTIVE: _____

FIRST NAME OF MAN IN ROOM: _____

FIRST NAME OF WOMAN IN ROOM: _____

ADJECTIVE: _____

ADVERB: _____

NOUN: _____

NOUN: _____

NOUN: _____

NOUN: _____

NOUN: _____

A NUMBER: _____

NOUN: _____

A LIQUID: _____

EXCLAMATION: _____

NOUN: _____

AN ADULT WESTERN

Tex _____, the marshall of Dodge City, rode
   LAST NAME OF MAN IN ROOM

into town. He sat _____ in the saddle, ready for trouble.
                    ADVERB

He knew that his _____ enemy, _____
                   ADJECTIVE   FIRST NAME OF MAN IN ROOM

the Kid, was in town. The Kid was in love with Tex's horse,

_____.
FIRST NAME OF WOMAN IN ROOM

   Suddenly the Kid came out of the _____ Nugget
                                      ADJECTIVE

Saloon. "Draw Tex!" he yelled _____.
                               ADVERB

   Tex reached for his _____, but before he could get it
                         NOUN

out of his _____, the Kid fired twice, hitting Tex in the
             NOUN

_____ and the _____. As Tex fell, he pulled
     NOUN   NOUN

his own _____ and shot the Kid _____
            NOUN   A NUMBER

times in the _____. The Kid dropped in a pool of
                NOUN

_____.
   A LIQUID

"_____!" Tex said, "I hated to do it, but he
        EXCLAMATION

was on the wrong side of the _____."
                               NOUN

From *Son of Mad Libs*® ● Copyright © 1988 Price Stem Sloan, Inc.,
A member of The Putnam & Grosset Group, New York, New York.

MAD LIBS® is fun to play with friends, but you can also play it by yourself! To begin with, DO NOT look at the story on the page below. Fill in the blanks on this page with the words called for. Then, using the words you've selected, fill in the blank spaces in the story.
Now you've created your own hilarious MAD LIB!

"THE FAMILY SPAT"

NAME OF GIRL IN ROOM:_____

NAME OF BOY IN ROOM:_____

PLURAL NOUN:_____

NOUN:_____

VERB (PAST TENSE):_____

PLURAL NOUN:_____

NOUN:_____

VERB:_____

VERB:_____

NOUN:_____

PART OF BODY:_____

VERB:_____

NOUN:_____

VERB ENDING IN "ING":_____

VERB:_____

PLURAL NOUN:_____

PART OF BODY:_____

"THE FAMILY SPAT"

To be read by _____ and _____.
                 NAME OF GIRL IN ROOM   NAME OF BOY IN ROOM

WIFE: Honey, I can't find the _____.
                                        PLURAL NOUN

HUSBAND: I put them in the _____ the last time I
                                      NOUN

_____ them.
  VERB (PAST TENSE)

WIFE: You always lose the _____.
                                     PLURAL NOUN

Why don't you put them back on the _____?
                                            NOUN

HUSBAND: Well, you are always forgetting to _____,
                                                        VERB

and that is worse than anything I do.

WIFE: What about the time you forgot to _____
                                                    VERB

the dog, and we had to take it to the _____
                                               NOUN

so that it could have its _____
                                 PART OF BODY

put in a splint. Poor thing, it has never been able to

_____ since then.
       VERB

HUSBAND: Well, that would have never happened if you hadn't left

for a week at your favorite _____.
                                    NOUN

When you leave, I do all the house _____.
                                           VERB ENDING IN "ING"

WIFE: Well, I suppose that is true. Why don't we get a maid,

then you will never _____ the
                            VERB

_____ again and the dog will not break
     PLURAL NOUN

the other _____.
                 PART OF BODY

MAD LIBS® is fun to play with friends, but you can also play it by yourself! To begin with, DO NOT look at the story on the page below. Fill in the blanks on this page with the words called for. Then, using the words you've selected, fill in the blank spaces in the story.

Now you've created your own hilarious MAD LIB!

LETTER RECEIVED BY THE FATHER OF

A MARRIAGEABLE DAUGHTER

NAME OF MAN IN ROOM: _____

ADJECTIVE: _____

FIRST NAME OF WOMAN IN ROOM: _____

NOUN: _____

NOUN: _____

NOUN: _____

PLURAL NOUN: _____

NOUN: _____

ADJECTIVE: _____

NUMBER: _____

NOUN: _____

GEOGRAPHICAL LOCATION: _____

ADJECTIVE: _____

ADJECTIVE: _____

NOUN: _____

NAME OF MAN IN ROOM: _____

LETTER RECEIVED BY THE FATHER
OF A MARRIAGEABLE DAUGHTER

Dear _____,
                NAME OF MAN IN ROOM

I am in love with your _____ daughter
                                    ADJECTIVE

_____ and I would like to ask for her
FIRST NAME OF WOMAN IN ROOM

_____ in marriage. She is my idea of a perfect
        NOUN

_____. She is the only _____ I have ever
        NOUN   NOUN

loved and I want her to be the mother of my _____. At
                                                        PLURAL NOUN

present I am employed as an assistant_____ and I make
                                                NOUN

a/an _____ salary of_____ dollars a week. I
            ADJECTIVE   NUMBER

have a split-level_____ picked out in_____
                        NOUN   GEOGRAPHICAL LOCATION

that we can live in. If you give your permission, I promise to make

her _____ and to be a/an _____
        ADJECTIVE   ADJECTIVE

_____.
        NOUN

Signed: _____
                        NAME OF MAN IN ROOM

MAD LIBS® is fun to play with friends, but you can also play it by yourself!
To begin with, DO NOT look at the story on the page below. Fill in the blanks
on this page with the words called for. Then, using the words you've selected, fill
in the blank spaces in the story.
Now you've created your own hilarious MAD LIB!

A COMMERCIAL MESSAGE FROM THE SPONSOR

ADJECTIVE: _____

ADJECTIVE: _____

ADJECTIVE: _____

NUMBER: _____

LIQUID: _____

ADJECTIVE: _____

NAME OF A TOOTHPASTE: _____

ADJECTIVE: _____

ADJECTIVE: _____

ADJECTIVE: _____

NOUN: _____

ADJECTIVE: _____

PLURAL NOUN: _____

COLOR: _____

NOUN: _____

NOUN: _____

A COMMERCIAL MESSAGE
FROM THE SPONSOR

Friends, have you noticed that your teeth are starting to look

_____ and _____?
   ADJECTIVE   ADJECTIVE

That's because you've been using the wrong toothpaste. Chomp

Toothpaste will make your teeth _____ after only
              ADJECTIVE

_____ brushings. That's because Chomp Toothpaste
  NUMBER

contains "Hex-a-chlor-a-_____," a secret ingredient
             LIQUID

known to your _____ druggist as _____.
      ADJECTIVE   NAME OF A TOOTHPASTE

Chomp attacks the _____ acids in your mouth and
         ADJECTIVE

leaves your breath _____ and _____. It will
       ADJECTIVE   ADJECTIVE

make your _____ feel _____ and will also
     NOUN   ADJECTIVE

stimulate your _____. Always keep the familiar
       PLURAL NOUN

_____ tube of Chomp handy in your _____.
  COLOR   NOUN

And now, back to our western program, "Have _____,
                                NOUN

Will Travel!"

MAD LIBS® is fun to play with friends, but you can also play it by yourself! To begin with, DO NOT look at the story on the page below. Fill in the blanks on this page with the words called for. Then, using the words you've selected, fill in the blank spaces in the story.
Now you've created your own hilarious MAD LIB!

NEW YEAR'S RESOLUTIONS

NAME OF PERSON IN ROOM:_____

VERB:_____

NUMBER:_____

NUMBER:_____

NOUN:_____

ADJECTIVE:_____

NAME OF PERSON IN ROOM:_____

ADJECTIVE:_____

NOUN:_____

NUMBER:_____

ADJECTIVE:_____

NOUN:_____

NOUN:_____

VERB:_____

NUMBER:_____

NUMBER:_____

ADJECTIVE:_____

PLURAL NOUN:_____

PERSON IN ROOM:_____

NOUN:_____

NUMBER:_____

NEW YEAR'S RESOLUTIONS

1. I, _____, will _____
   NAME OF PERSON IN ROOM   VERB

   every day at the gym for at least _____
                                              NUMBER

   minutes.

2. At the dinner table, I will eat only _____
                                                 NUMBER

   servings of _____.
                    NOUN

3. I will watch only _____ television shows.
                            ADJECTIVE

4. I will tell _____ that I think he (she) is a/an
                NAME OF PERSON IN ROOM

   _____ _____.
        ADJECTIVE   NOUN

5. I will ask my boss for a/an _____-dollar raise.
                                        NUMBER

6. I will admit that I have a/an _____ personality.
                                       ADJECTIVE

7. I will take my _____ to _____
                        NOUN   NOUN

   at least once a month.

8. I will _____ one book every _____
                  VERB   NUMBER

   weeks.

9. I will try to lose at least _____ pounds.
                                        NUMBER

10. I will return the _____ _____
                            ADJECTIVE   PLURAL NOUN

    I borrowed from _____.
                        PERSON IN ROOM

11. I will get on a _____ and only spend
                          NOUN

    _____ dollars a month.
          NUMBER

MAD LIBS® is fun to play with friends, but you can also play it by yourself! To begin with, DO NOT look at the story on the page below. Fill in the blanks on this page with the words called for. Then, using the words you've selected, fill in the blank spaces in the story.
Now you've created your own hilarious MAD LIB!

ADVERTISEMENT

NOUN:_____

NUMBER:_____

VERB ENDING IN "ING":_____

VERB ENDING IN "ING":_____

VERB ENDING IN "ING":_____

NOUN:_____

ADJECTIVE:_____

PLURAL NOUN:_____

NOUN:_____

ADJECTIVE:_____

NOUN:_____

ADJECTIVE:_____

VERB:_____

PERSON IN ROOM:_____

NOUN:_____

NOUN:_____

NOUN:_____

NOUN:_____

SILLY WORD:_____

NOUN:_____

ADVERTISEMENT

Seeking a new career? Be a _____ or just

NOUN

look like one! In just _____ sessions, we can have you

NUMBER

_____, _____, and _____

VERB ENDING IN "ING"   VERB ENDING IN "ING"   VERB ENDING IN "ING"

like a top-paying _____. Opportunities in this

NOUN

_____ field are limitless. There is no fee! Just come in

ADJECTIVE

for a free consultation. Our expert _____ will

PLURAL NOUN

analyze your _____ and determine your poten-

NOUN

tial for success in this _____ field. Use your

ADJECTIVE

natural _____ to earn _____

NOUN   ADJECTIVE

money and have time to _____ your dreams too.

VERB

Just ask _____ who came to us look-

PERSON IN ROOM

ing like a _____ out of _____ and in

NOUN   NOUN

just ten days we improved his/her _____ 100%.

NOUN

We even corrected his/her horrible _____. It

NOUN

was just in the nick of time because the _____ Squad

SILLY WORD

was ready to ban him/her from the _____. Don't

NOUN

wait another day. Time is running out.

MAD LIBS® is fun to play with friends, but you can also play it by yourself!
To begin with, DO NOT look at the story on the page below. Fill in the blanks
on this page with the words called for. Then, using the words you've selected, fill
in the blank spaces in the story.
Now you've created your own hilarious MAD LIB!

POLICE CALL

NAME OF BOY IN ROOM: _____

ADJECTIVE: _____

NOUN: _____

NOUN: _____

A PLACE: _____

NOUN: _____

NOUN: _____

NOUN: _____

ADJECTIVE: _____

NOUN: _____

ADJECTIVE: _____

A WEAPON: _____

NOUN: _____

NOUN: _____

ADJECTIVE: _____

POLICE CALL

Calling all cars...calling all cars! Be on the lookout for

_____. He is wearing a/an _____
NAME OF PERSON IN ROOM   ADJECTIVE

suit, a gray _____, and carrying an old brown
                NOUN

_____. He was last seen in the vicinity of _____
NOUN   A PLACE

waving a loaded _____. He is charged with holding up a
                 NOUN

candy store and running off with the owner's_____. He
                                              NOUN

is also accused of stealing a 1955 _____ and a/an
                                    NOUN

_____ _____. It is advisable to approach
ADJECTIVE   NOUN

this man with _____ caution as he has been known to
              ADJECTIVE

carry a loaded _____. He uses the alias 'Henry the
               A WEAPON

_____' and has been known to disguise himself as a/an
NOUN

_____. Watch out for this _____ ____ criminal.
NOUN   ADJECTIVE

That is all.

MAD LIBS® is fun to play with friends, but you can also play it by yourself!
To begin with, DO NOT look at the story on the page below. Fill in the blanks
on this page with the words called for. Then, using the words you've selected, fill
in the blank spaces in the story.
Now you've created your own hilarious MAD LIB!

HOROSCOPE

NOUN: _____

ADJECTIVE: _____

PLURAL NOUN: _____

ADJECTIVE: _____

SILLY WORD: _____

NOUN: _____

PLURAL NOUN: _____

PLURAL NOUN: _____

ADJECTIVE: _____

PLURAL NOUN: _____

ADJECTIVE: _____

ADJECTIVE: _____

ADJECTIVE: _____

PLURAL NOUN: _____

ADJECTIVE: _____

ADJECTIVE: _____

PLURAL NOUN: _____

ADJECTIVE: _____

ADJECTIVE: _____

HOROSCOPE

Those born under the planetary sign of the _____

NOUN

possess _____ personalities and are forever

ADJECTIVE

searching for new _____ to conquer. This is a

PLURAL NOUN

more or less _____ month for you because the

ADJECTIVE

planet _____ is directly over your

SILLY WORD

_____ and Mercury is influencing your

NOUN

_____. This means you should avoid eating

PLURAL NOUN

_____ and stay away from anybody with

PLURAL NOUN

_____ _____. During the coming year

ADJECTIVE   PLURAL NOUN

you will find conditions getting _____ due

ADJECTIVE

to your _____ outlook on life and your

ADJECTIVE

_____ attitude toward _____.

ADJECTIVE   PLURAL NOUN

You are best suited to a/an _____ mate with

ADJECTIVE

_____ _____

ADJECTIVE   PLURAL NOUN

and a/an _____ complexion, which means, of

ADJECTIVE

course, that you can look forward to a really _____ life.

ADJECTIVE

From *Son of Mad Libs*® ● Copyright © 1988 Price Stern Sloan, Inc.,

A member of The Putnam & Grosset Group, New York, New York.

MAD LIBS® is fun to play with friends, but you can also play it by yourself! To begin with, DO NOT look at the story on the page below. Fill in the blanks on this page with the words called for. Then, using the words you've selected, fill in the blank spaces in the story.

Now you've created your own hilarious MAD LIB!

POLITICAL SPEECH

ADJECTIVE: _____

ADJECTIVE: _____

PLURAL NOUN: _____

PLURAL NOUN: _____

ADJECTIVE: _____

NOUN: _____

NOUN: _____

PLURAL NOUN: _____

ADJECTIVE: _____

NAME OF PERSON IN ROOM: _____

ADJECTIVE: _____

NOUN: _____

ADJECTIVE: _____

NOUN: _____

PLURAL NOUN: _____

PLURAL NOUN: _____

ADJECTIVE: _____

ADJECTIVE: _____

ADJECTIVE: _____

POLITICAL SPEECH

Ladies and gentlemen, on this _____ occasion it is a
ADJECTIVE

privilege to address such a/an _____-looking group of
ADJECTIVE

_____. I can tell from your smiling _____
PLURAL NOUN   PLURAL NOUN

that you will support my _____ program in the coming
ADJECTIVE

election. I promise that, if elected, there will be a/an _____
NOUN

in every _____ and two _____ in every
NOUN   PLURAL NOUN

garage. I want to warn you against my _____ opponent,
ADJECTIVE

Mr. _____. This man is nothing but a/an
NAME OF PERSON IN ROOM

_____ _____. He has a/an _____
ADJECTIVE   NOUN   ADJECTIVE

character and is working _____ in glove with the
NOUN

criminal element. If elected, I promise to eliminate vice. I will keep

the _____ off the city's streets. I will keep crooks from
PLURAL NOUN

dipping their _____ in the public till. I promise you
PLURAL NOUN

_____ government, _____ taxes, and
ADJECTIVE   ADJECTIVE

_____ schools.
ADJECTIVE

From *Son of Mad Libs*® ● Copyright © 1988 Price Stern Sloan, Inc..

A member of The Putnam & Grosset Group, New York, New York.

MAD LIBS® is fun to play with friends, but you can also play it by yourself! To begin with, DO NOT look at the story on the page below. Fill in the blanks on this page with the words called for. Then, using the words you've selected, fill in the blank spaces in the story.
Now you've created your own hilarious MAD LIB!

PROVERBS

PLURAL NOUN:_____

A LIQUID:_____

ADJECTIVE:_____

PLURAL NOUN:_____

PLURAL NOUN:_____

NOUN:_____

PLURAL NOUN:_____

ADJECTIVE:_____

NOUN:_____

NOUN:_____

NOUN:_____

VERB (PRESENT TENSE):_____

VERB (PRESENT TENSE):_____

NOUN:_____

A NUMBER:_____

ADJECTIVE:_____

ADJECTIVE:_____

NOUN:_____

ADJECTIVE:_____

ADJECTIVE:_____

NOUN:_____

NOUN:_____

NOUN:_____

PROVERBS

Too many _____ spoil the _____.
     PLURAL NOUN   **A LIQUID**

People who live in _____ houses shouldn't throw
      ADJECTIVE

_____.
  PLURAL NOUN

The shortest distance between two _____ is a
        PLURAL NOUN

straight _____.
    NOUN

Love of _____ is the root of all evil.
    PLURAL NOUN

A/An _____ stone gathers no _____.
   ADJECTIVE   **NOUN**

A/An _____ a day keeps the _____
   NOUN   **NOUN**

away.

He who _____ last _____ best.
  VERB (PRESENT TENSE)   **VERB (PRESENT TENSE)**

A/An _____ in time saves _____.
   NOUN   **NUMBER**

You can't keep a/an _____ man down.
      ADJECTIVE

You can't teach a/an _____ _____
      ADJECTIVE   **NOUN**

new tricks.

Life is _____, life is _____, and
   ADJECTIVE   **ADJECTIVE**

the _____ is not the goal.
   NOUN

The way to a man's _____ is through his
      NOUN

_____.
  NOUN

MAD LIBS® is fun to play with friends, but you can also play it by yourself! To begin with, DO NOT look at the story on the page below. Fill in the blanks on this page with the words called for. Then, using the words you've selected, fill in the blank spaces in the story.
Now you've created your own hilarious MAD LIB!

FATHER GOOSE RHYMES

NOUN: _____

ADJECTIVE: _____

NOUN: _____

NOUN: _____

ADJECTIVE: _____

ADJECTIVE: _____

NOUN: _____

CONTAINER: _____

NOUN: _____

NOUN: _____

ADJECTIVE: _____

ADJECTIVE: _____

ADJECTIVE: _____

ADJECTIVE: _____

VERB (PAST TENSE): _____

PLURAL NOUN: _____

FATHER GOOSE RHYMES

Old Mother Hubbard went to the _____
                                    NOUN

To get her _____ _____ a bone.
              ADJECTIVE   NOUN

When she got there, the _____ was _____,
                          NOUN   ADJECTIVE

And so her _____ dog had none.
              ADJECTIVE

Jack and Jill went up the _____
                            NOUN

To fetch a/an _____ of water.
                CONTAINER

Jack fell down and broke his _____,
                               NOUN

And Jill came tumbling after.

There was a little girl and she had a little curl

Right in the middle of her _____.
                             NOUN

And when she was _____, she was very, very _____,
                    ADJECTIVE   ADJECTIVE

And when she was bad, she was _____.
                                ADJECTIVE

There was a/an _____ woman
                 ADJECTIVE

Who _____ in a shoe.
      VERB (PAST TENSE)

She had so many _____
                  PLURAL NOUN

She didn't know what to do.

MAD LIBS® is fun to play with friends, but you can also play it by yourself! To begin with, DO NOT look at the story on the page below. Fill in the blanks on this page with the words called for. Then, using the words you've selected, fill in the blank spaces in the story.
Now you've created your own hilarious MAD LIB!

MORE FATHER GOOSE RHYMES

NOUN: _____

NOUN: _____

NOUN THAT RHYMES WITH "MOON": _____

NOUN THAT RHYMES WITH "MOON": _____

NOUN: _____

NOUN THAT RHYMES WITH "DAY": _____

NOUN: _____

MUSICAL INSTRUMENT: _____

NOUN: _____

NOUN: _____

ADJECTIVE: _____

NOUN: _____

ANIMAL: _____

NOUN: _____

NOUN: _____

VERB THAT RHYMES WITH "SNOW": _____

MORE FATHER GOOSE RHYMES

Hi, diddle, diddle, the _____ and the fiddle,
                          NOUN

The _____ jumped over the _____.
        NOUN   NOUN THAT RHYMES WITH "MOON"

The little dog laughed to see such sport,

And the dish ran away with the _____.
                                 NOUN THAT RHYMES WITH "MOON"

★★★★★

Little Miss Muffet sat on a/an _____,
                                 NOUN

Eating her curds and _____.
                       NOUN THAT RHYMES WITH "DAY"

Along came a/an _____ and sat down beside her
                   NOUN

And frightened Miss Muffet away.

★★★★★

Little Boy Blue come blow your _____.
                                 MUSICAL INSTRUMENT

The sheep's in the _____,
                     NOUN

The cow's in the _____.
                   NOUN

Where is the _____ boy who looks after the sheep?
               ADJECTIVE

He's under the _____, fast asleep.
                 NOUN

★★★★★

Mary had a little _____.
                    ANIMAL

Its _____ was white as snow.
      NOUN

And everywhere that Mary went

Her _____ was sure to _____
      NOUN   VERB THAT RHYMES WITH "SNOW"

MAD LIBS® is fun to play with friends, but you can also play it by yourself!
To begin with, DO NOT look at the story on the page below. Fill in the blanks
on this page with the words called for. Then, using the words you've selected, fill
in the blank spaces in the story.
Now you've created your own hilarious MAD LIB!

BIRD WATCHING AND VICE VERSA

PLURAL NOUN: _____

ADJECTIVE: _____

ADJECTIVE: _____

NOUN: _____

FUNNY NOISE: _____

VERB: _____

NUMBER: _____

ADJECTIVE: _____

ADJECTIVE: _____

NOUN: _____

PLURAL NOUN: _____

NOUN: _____

ADJECTIVE: _____

ADJECTIVE: _____

BIRD WATCHING AND VICE VERSA

Bird watching can be more fun than a barrel of _____.

PLURAL NOUN

Our _____ feathered friends are everywhere, waiting to

ADJECTIVE

be watched. An interesting bird to start with is the _____

ADJECTIVE

oriole, which builds its nest in _____ trees. Early in

NOUN

spring we hear the oriole give its mating call, which sounds like this:

"_____." Then the male and female get together and

FUNNY NOISE

_____. Later, the female lays _____ eggs.

VERB   NUMBER

Isn't that _____? Another fascinating bird is the

ADJECTIVE

_____-breasted nuthatch. The nuthatch is very tame.

ADJECTIVE

He will fly down and land right on your _____, and eat

NOUN

out of your _____. Other birds to watch out for are the

PLURAL NOUN

red-crested _____, the _____-necked thrush,

NOUN   ADJECTIVE

and the yellow-bellied _____ sucker. Now that you

ADJECTIVE

know something about birds – get out there and watch!

MAD LIBS® is fun to play with friends, but you can also play it by yourself!
To begin with, DO NOT look at the story on the page below. Fill in the blanks
on this page with the words called for. Then, using the words you've selected, fill
in the blank spaces in the story.
Now you've created your own hilarious MAD LIB!

A BASEBALL BROADCAST

COLOR: _____

PLURAL NOUN: _____

ADJECTIVE: _____

CELEBRITY: _____

ADJECTIVE: _____

NOUN: _____

NUMBER: _____

NUMBER: _____

NOUN: _____

ADJECTIVE: _____

CELEBRITY: _____

CELEBRITY: _____

ADJECTIVE: _____

NOUN: _____

CELEBRITY: _____

ADJECTIVE: _____ _____

A BASEBALL BROADCAST

Ladies and gentlemen, this is _____ Barber, your
COLOR

sportscaster, bringing you the last inning of the game between the

Cleveland _____ and the _____ Yankees.
PLURAL NOUN ADJECTIVE

_____ is pitching for the Yankees. Here's the pitch! It's
CELEBRITY

a low _____ ball that just cuts the inside of the
ADJECTIVE

_____ for a strike. That makes the count _____
NOUN NUMBER

strikes and _____ balls. Now here's the next pitch. The
NUMBER

batter swings and connects. It's a long, high _____ out
NOUN

to _____ field. But _____ is coming up fast
ADJECTIVE CELEBRITY

and has it for the second out. The next batter up is _____,
CELEBRITY

the Cleveland _____-stop. Here's the pitch . . . and it's
ADJECTIVE

hit . . . a short ground ball to third _____.
NOUN

_____ scoops it up and throws it to first base for the out,
CELEBRITY

and the game is over. And the Yankees move into second place in the

_____ League!
ADJECTIVE

MAD LIBS® is fun to play with friends, but you can also play it by yourself!
To begin with, DO NOT look at the story on the page below. Fill in the blanks
on this page with the words called for. Then, using the words you've selected, fill
in the blank spaces in the story.
Now you've created your own hilarious MAD LIB!

MOTHER AND SON

ADJECTIVE: _____

NOUN: _____

PLURAL NOUN: _____

PLURAL NOUN: _____

ADJECTIVE: _____

NOUN: _____

NOUN: _____

PLURAL NOUN: _____

CELEBRITY: _____

NOUN: _____

ADJECTIVE: _____

NOUN: _____

MOTHER AND SON

MOTHER: Junior, you come right inside. You're late, and your supper is getting _____.

ADJECTIVE

SON: Aw, Mom. I've been out playing _____ ball with some of the other _____.

NOUN

PLURAL NOUN

MOTHER: Well, get inside. And don't forget to wipe your muddy _____.

PLURAL NOUN

SON: Okay, Mom. Can I watch television while I eat? There's a/an _____ new show on.

ADJECTIVE

MOTHER: No, not while you're eating your _____.

NOUN

SON: But Mom! "Have _____ Will Travel" is on.

NOUN

MOTHER: No, sir. You've been watching too much television. You're liable to strain your _____.

PLURAL NOUN

SON: Gee whiz! That's my favorite program. It stars _____ as the gunslinger.

CELEBRITY

MOTHER: Never mind. Go and wash your _____.

NOUN

SON: Aw, Mom. I don't have to. I'm _____.

ADJECTIVE

MOTHER: Don't talk back to me, young man, or I'll have to speak to your _____.

NOUN

MAD LIBS® is fun to play with friends, but you can also play it by yourself! To begin with, DO NOT look at the story on the page below. Fill in the blanks on this page with the words called for. Then, using the words you've selected, fill in the blank spaces in the story.
Now you've created your own hilarious MAD LIB!

WEATHER REPORT

GEOGRAPHIC LOCATION:_____

ADJECTIVE:_____

PLURAL NOUN:_____

ADJECTIVE:_____

PLURAL NOUN:_____

NUMBER:_____

NUMBER:_____

NOUN:_____

ITEMS FROM A GOSSIP COLUMN

WOMAN IN ROOM:_____

MAN IN ROOM:_____

PLURAL NOUN:_____

MAN IN ROOM:_____

WOMAN IN ROOM:_____

SAME WOMAN IN ROOM:_____

NOUN:_____

WEATHER REPORT

Here is tomorrow's weather report for _____ and
                                        GEOGRAPHIC LOCATION

vicinity. Early tomorrow a/an _____ front will collide
                              ADJECTIVE

with a mass of hot _____ moving from the north. This
                   PLURAL NOUN

means we can expect _____ winds and occasional
                    ADJECTIVE

_____ by late afternoon. Wind velocity will be
PLURAL NOUN

_____ miles an hour and the high temperature should
NUMBER

be around _____ degrees. So if you're going out, you'd
          NUMBER

better wear your _____.
                 NOUN

ITEMS FROM A GOSSIP COLUMN

_____ and her husband, _____ were
WOMAN IN ROOM   MAN IN ROOM

seen last night at the Twenty-Three Club holding _____.
                                                 PLURAL NOUN

Could it be reconciliation? The International heartthrob,

_____ and the glamorous top model,
MAN IN ROOM

_____, are expecting their first baby in
WOMAN IN ROOM

November. _____ is denying stork rumors, but yester-
          SAME WOMAN IN ROOM

day she was seen buying a maternity _____.
                                    NOUN

MAD LIBS® is fun to play with friends, but you can also play it by yourself! To begin with, DO NOT look at the story on the page below. Fill in the blanks on this page with the words called for. Then, using the words you've selected, fill in the blank spaces in the story.

Now you've created your own hilarious MAD LIB!

SUPERSTITIONS

ADVERB: _____

PLURAL NOUN: _____

ADJECTIVE: _____

PLURAL NOUN: _____

PART OF BODY: _____

ANIMAL: _____

NOUN: _____

A NUMBER: _____

ADJECTIVE: _____

VERB (PRESENT TENSE): _____

PART OF BODY: _____

ANIMAL: _____

GEOGRAPHICAL LOCATION: _____

SOMETHING TO EAT: _____

PART OF BODY: _____

SUPERSTITIONS

Although we believe ourselves to be _____ civilized,
ADVERB

most of us are really _____ at heart because we still
PLURAL NOUN

believe in _____ superstitions that began while man still
ADJECTIVE

lived in _____. Some of these superstitions are:
PLURAL NOUN

1. If you spill salt, throw some over your left _____.
PART OF BODY

2. If a black _____ runs in front of you, you are in
ANIMAL

trouble.

3. If you break a/an _____, you will have _____
NOUN A NUMBER

years of _____ luck.
ADJECTIVE

4. Never _____ under a ladder.
VERB (PRESENT TENSE)

5. If your _____ itches, it means you will have a
PART OF BODY

visitor.

6. If you hear a/an _____ howl at midnight, someone
ANIMAL

in your family will end up in _____.
GEOGRAPHICAL LOCATION

7. If you want to keep vampires away, always wear a/an

_____ on a string around your _____.
SOMETHING TO EAT PART OF BODY

From *Sooper Dooper Mad Libs*® ● Copyright © 1988 Price Stern Sloan, Inc.,
A member of The Putnam & Grosset Group, New York, New York.

MAD LIBS® is fun to play with friends, but you can also play it by yourself! To begin with, DO NOT look at the story on the page below. Fill in the blanks on this page with the words called for. Then, using the words you've selected, fill in the blank spaces in the story.

Now you've created your own hilarious MAD LIB!

CHINESE DINNER

ADJECTIVE: _____

ADJECTIVE: _____

CELEBRITY: _____

ADJECTIVE: _____

NOUN: _____

ADJECTIVE: _____

ADJECTIVE: _____

NOUN: _____

NOUN: _____

FOOD: _____

FOOD: _____

NOUN: _____

FOOD: _____

ADJECTIVE: _____

CHINESE DINNER

I recently had dinner at a new Chinese restaurant. The cooking is

_____ and the service is _____. The owner
ADJECTIVE   ADJECTIVE

of the restaurant, _____, suggested that for my first
CELEBRITY

course I have sweet and _____ spare ribs, which is a
ADJECTIVE

specialty of the _____. They were _____.
NOUN   ADJECTIVE

For the next course, I was served a/an _____ _____
ADJECTIVE   NOUN

soup. The main course consisted of Egg Foo _____,
NOUN

lobster in _____ sauce, and pressed _____.
FOOD   FOOD

For dessert, I ordered those famous Chinese _____
NOUN

cookies with sliced _____. But whenever I eat Chinese
FOOD

food, an hour later I feel _____ again.
ADJECTIVE

From *Sooper Dooper Mad Libs* ● Copyright © 1988 Price Stern Sloan, Inc.,
A member of The Putnam & Grosset Group, New York, New York.

MAD LIBS® is fun to play with friends, but you can also play it by yourself!
To begin with, DO NOT look at the story on the page below. Fill in the blanks
on this page with the words called for. Then, using the words you've selected, fill
in the blank spaces in the story.
Now you've created your own hilarious MAD LIB!

HAMLET

CELEBRITY: _____

ADJECTIVE: _____

NOUN: _____

LIQUID: _____

NOUN: _____

NOUN: _____

PLURAL NOUN: _____

PLURAL NOUN: _____

PLURAL NOUN: _____

PLURAL NOUN: _____

VERB: _____

VERB: _____

VERB: _____

NOUN: _____

HAMLET

This is the soliloquy from the play, "Hamlet," written by

_____. In the third act of this _____
            CELEBRITY   ADJECTIVE

play, Hamlet, who is sometimes called "the melancholy _____,"
                                                          NOUN

is suspicious of his stepfather and hires some actors to act out a

scene in which a king is killed when someone pours _____
                                                       LIQUID

into his _____. First, however, he declaims: To be or not
           NOUN

to be: that is the _____: Whether 'tis nobler in the mind
                      NOUN

to suffer the _____ and _____ of outrageous
                PLURAL NOUN   PLURAL NOUN

fortune, or to take arms against a sea of _____, and by
                                              PLURAL NOUN

opposing end them. To die: to sleep; no more; and by a sleep to say

we end the heart-ache and the thousand natural _____
                                                   PLURAL NOUN

that flesh is heir to, 'tis a consummation devoutly to be wish'd. To die,

to _____; to _____: perchance to
        VERB   VERB

_____: ay, there's the _____.
     VERB   NOUN

From *Sooper Dooper Mad Libs*® ● Copyright © 1988 Price Stern Sloan, Inc.,

A member of The Putnam & Grosset Group, New York, New York.

MAD LIBS® is fun to play with friends, but you can also play it by yourself!
To begin with, DO NOT look at the story on the page below. Fill in the blanks
on this page with the words called for. Then, using the words you've selected, fill
in the blank spaces in the story.
Now you've created your own hilarious MAD LIB!

HAPPY BIRTHDAY! ·

NAME OF GIRL IN ROOM: _____

NOUN: _____

ADJECTIVE: _____

NOUN: _____

NUMBER: _____

BOY IN ROOM: _____

NOUN: _____

NOUN: _____

PLURAL NOUN: _____

ADJECTIVE: _____

NOUN: _____

ADJECTIVE: _____

PLURAL NOUN: _____

NOUN: _____

HAPPY BIRTHDAY!

Friends, this gathering is a surprise party for _____.
NAME OF GIRL IN ROOM

We are here to celebrate her _____. All of her most
NOUN

_____ friends are here, including me, her devoted and
ADJECTIVE

faithful _____. I must say that she doesn't look a day
NOUN

over _____. Naturally, we have some presents.
NUMBER

_____ brought her a beautiful copper _____
BOY IN ROOM   NOUN

that she can wear on her lovely _____. And our hostess
NOUN

got her a dozen _____ that she can hang in her
PLURAL NOUN

bathroom. And we had the bakery send up a huge _____
ADJECTIVE

_____ with candles on it. We all want to wish her a very
NOUN

_____ birthday and many happy _____.
ADJECTIVE   PLURAL NOUN

Now let's all sing together: "Happy _____ to you!"
NOUN

(Editor's Note: Sing until all are exhausted.)

MAD LIBS® is fun to play with friends, but you can also play it by
yourself! To begin with, DO NOT look at the story on the page below. Fill
in the blanks on this page with the words called for. Then, using the words
you've selected, fill in the blank spaces in the story.
Now you've created your own hilarious MAD LIB!

WAITRESS AND CUSTOMER

NOUN:_____

AN ANIMAL:_____

NOUN:_____

PLURAL NOUN:_____

ADJECTIVE:_____

NOUN:_____

ADJECTIVE:_____

ADJECTIVE:_____

NOUN:_____

NOUN:_____

ADJECTIVE:_____

NOUN:_____

ADJECTIVE:_____

LIQUID:_____

WAITRESS AND CUSTOMER

Scene: A restaurant (where else?)

CUSTOMER: Oh, waitress! Would you please bring me a

_____, I want to see what today's
NOUN

special is.

WAITRESS: Today's special is _____ sauted in
AN ANIMAL

cream of _____ soup. Does that
NOUN

sound good?

CUSTOMER: No, I'll have the roast prime _____
PLURAL NOUN

of beef with the _____ pudding.
ADJECTIVE

WAITRESS: We're out of that. How about a sizzling sirloin

_____ and a/an _____
NOUN   ADJECTIVE

green salad?

CUSTOMER: No thanks, I'd rather have the _____
ADJECTIVE

fried chicken.

WAITRESS: Sorry, but we're out of that, too. How about fried

_____?
NOUN

CUSTOMER: No thanks. Do you have any roast Long Island

_____?
NOUN

WAITRESS: No, but why don't you try our _____
ADJECTIVE

goulash with homemade _____
NOUN

sauce?

CUSTOMER: Oh, never mind. Just bring me a/an _____
ADJECTIVE

egg sandwich and a cup of black _____!
LIQUID

MAD LIBS® is fun to play with friends, but you can also play it by yourself! To begin with, DO NOT look at the story on the page below. Fill in the blanks on this page with the words called for. Then, using the words you've selected, fill in the blank spaces in the story.
Now you've created your own hilarious MAD LIB!

LETTER TO A LOVELORN COLUMNIST

NUMBER:_____

VERB (PRESENT):_____

VERB (PAST TENSE):_____

NOUN:_____

NOUN:_____

PLURAL NOUN:_____

ADJECTIVE:_____

PART OF BODY:_____

ADJECTIVE:_____

NAME OF WOMAN IN ROOM:_____

REPLY FROM MISS LONELYHEARTS

ADJECTIVE:_____

VERB ENDING IN "ING":_____

VERB ENDING IN "ING":_____

PURAL NOUN:_____

VERB:_____

NOUN:_____

NUMBER:_____

LETTER TO A LOVELORN COLUMNIST

Dear Miss Lonelyhearts:

I've been engaged to the same man for _____ years. He
                                              NUMBER

keeps telling me he _____ me, but we need to wait to get
                       VERB (PRESENT TENSE)

_____ until he makes more _____. If we
VERB (PAST TENSE)   NOUN

marry now, we will have to _____ with my mother and
                                  NOUN

eat _____ every day. But isn't _____
        PLURAL NOUN   ADJECTIVE

love worth that? Should I put my _____ down and set a
                                      PART OF BODY

date, or just continue to be _____?
                                 ADJECTIVE

Signed,

_____
NAME OF WOMAN IN ROOM

REPLY FROM MISS LONELYHEARTS

Dear Young Lady:

Don't do anything _____. Something worth
                        ADJECTIVE

_____ is worth _____ for. I don't think
VERB ENDING IN "ING"   VERB ENDING IN "ING"

eating _____ with the man you
            PLURAL NOUN

_____ is bad, but eating _____ and
     VERB   NOUN

living _____ miles away from mother is better.
           NUMBER

Signed,

Miss Lonelyhearts

MAD LIBS® is fun to play with friends, but you can also play it by yourself! To begin with, DO NOT look at the story on the page below. Fill in the blanks on this page with the words called for. Then, using the words you've selected, fill in the blank spaces in the story.
Now you've created your own hilarious MAD LIB!

TOO MUCH FATHER GOOSE

ADJECTIVE: _____

NOUN: _____

PLURAL NOUN: _____

NOUN: _____

ADJECTIVE: _____

ADJECTIVE: _____

ADJECTIVE: _____

ADJECTIVE: _____

ADJECTIVE: _____

ADJECTIVE: _____

NOUN: _____

ADJECTIVE: _____

ADJECTIVE: _____

NOUN: _____

NOUN: _____

NOUN: _____

ADJECTIVE: _____

ADJECTIVE: _____

NOUN: _____

NOUN: _____

PLURAL NOUN: _____

TOO MUCH FATHER GOOSE

Three _____ mice. See how they run!
       ADJECTIVE

They all ran after the farmer's _____.
                                  NOUN

Who cut off their _____ with a carving _____
                   PLURAL NOUN   NOUN

Did you ever see such a sight in your life

As three _____ mice?
         ADJECTIVE
★★★★★
There was a crooked man and he went a/an _____ mile.
                                          ADJECTIVE

He found a/an _____
                              ADJECTIVE

against a/an _____ stile.
             ADJECTIVE

He bought a/an _____ cat, which caught a/an
                ADJECTIVE

_____ mouse.
   ADJECTIVE

And they all lived together in in a little crooked _____.
                                                    NOUN
★★★★★
_____ Jack Horner sat in the corner
   ADJECTIVE

Eating his _____ pie.
            ADJECTIVE

He stuck in his _____ and pulled out a/an _____
                 NOUN   NOUN

And said, "What a good _____ am I!"
                        NOUN
★★★★★
Old King Cole was a/an _____ old soul,
                        ADJECTIVE

A/An _____ old soul was he.
      ADJECTIVE

He called for his _____, and he called for his _____
                   NOUN   NOUN

And he called for his _____ three.

MAD LIBS® is fun to play with friends, but you can also play it by yourself! To begin with, DO NOT look at the story on the page below. Fill in the blanks on this page with the words called for. Then, using the words you've selected, fill in the blank spaces in the story.
Now you've created your own hilarious MAD LIB!

MEDICAL QUESTIONS AND ANSWERS

PERSON IN ROOM:_____

ANOTHER PERSON IN ROOM:_____

ADJECTIVE:_____

NOUN:_____

NOUN:_____

NOUN:_____

NOUN:_____

ADJECTIVE:_____

ADJECTIVE:_____

ADJECTIVE:_____

NOUN:_____

LIQUID:_____

PLURAL NOUN:_____

NUMBER:_____

BODY PART:_____

NOUN:_____

NOUN:_____

MEDICAL QUESTIONS AND ANSWERS

The Patient to be played by _____, the Doctor to be
PERSON IN ROOM

played by _____.
ANOTHER PERSON IN ROOM

PATIENT: Doctor, whenever I stand up I get a/an _____
ADJECTIVE

pain in my _____. Is this serious?
NOUN

DOCTOR: Sounds as if you have an inflammation of your

_____. You need an
NOUN

anti-_____ shot.
NOUN

PATIENT: Doctor, I'm thinking of having my _____
NOUN

removed. Is this a/an _____ operation?
ADJECTIVE

DOCTOR: No, the operation is quite _____, provid-
ADJECTIVE

ing you have _____ kidneys.
ADJECTIVE

PATIENT: What are the symptoms of an overactive

_____?
NOUN

DOCTOR: High _____ pressure. Also severe
LIQUID

_____ in the abdomen.
PLURAL NOUN

PATIENT: Doctor, is it possible for a/an _____- year-
NUMBER

old man to have a _____ attack?
BODY PART

DOCTOR: Only if he doesn't watch is _____ and eats
NOUN

too much _____.
NOUN

MAD LIBS® is fun to play with friends, but you can also play it by yourself! To begin with, DO NOT look at the story on the page below. Fill in the blanks on this page with the words called for. Then, using the words you've selected, fill in the blank spaces in the story.
Now you've created your own hilarious MAD LIB!

COUNTRY AND WESTERN MUSIC

ADJECTIVE: _____

ADJECTIVE: _____

CLOTHING (PLURAL): _____

PLURAL NOUN: _____

ANIMAL (PLURAL): _____

VERB ENDING IN "ING": _____

PART OF BODY: _____

VERB: _____

ADJECTIVE: _____

PLURAL NOUN: _____

PLURAL NOUN: _____

COUNTRY AND WESTERN

The most _____ music in the U.S. today is called
　　　　　　ADJECTIVE

"Country and _____" music. The musicians all wear
　　　　　　　ADJECTIVE

cowboy _____ and play electric _____.
　　　CLOTHING (PLURAL)　　　　　　　　　PLURAL NOUN

They sing about roping _____ and _____
　　　　　　　　ANIMAL (PLURAL)　　　　VERB ENDING IN "ING"

out in the stable. In a lot of songs the people end up with a broken

_____ and vow they will never _____
　　PART OF BODY　　　　　　　　　　　　　　VERB

again. Most country records are made in Nashville, Tennessee, the

home of the _____ Old Opry. Most cowboys are just
　　　　　ADJECTIVE

ordinary _____ who wear on big hats and tell even
　　　PLURAL NOUN

bigger _____.
　　PLURAL NOUN

MAD LIBS® is fun to play with friends, but you can also play it by yourself! To begin with, DO NOT look at the story on the page below. Fill in the blanks on this page with the words called for. Then, using the words you've selected, fill in the blank spaces in the story.
Now you've created your own hilarious MAD LIB!

SCHOOL DAYS

PLURAL NOUN: _____

PLURAL NOUN: _____

PLURAL NOUN: _____

ADJECTIVE: _____

NOUN: _____

NOUN: _____

AN ANIMAL: _____

NOUN: _____

LIQUID: _____

NOUN: _____

NOUN: _____

NOUN: _____

VERB (PAST TENSE): _____

NOUN: _____

VERB: _____

NOUN: _____

NOUN: _____

PLURAL NOUN: _____

PLURAL NOUN: _____

PART OF BODY (PLURAL): _____

SCHOOL DAYS

Things were different when I went to school. First of all, we didn't have

any _____ to do our math for us. We would add col-
　　　　　　PLURAL NOUN

umns of _____ to other columns of _____
　　　　　　PLURAL NOUN　　　　　　　　　　　　　　PLURAL NOUN

to master addition. We had to sit _____ when the
　　　　　　　　　　　　　　　　　　　　　ADJECTIVE

teacher lectured to us about American _____ and
　　　　　　　　　　　　　　　　　　　　　　　　　NOUN

English _____. Everyday at lunch we would eat
　　　　　　　NOUN

a _____ sandwich, a _____ and a glass
　　　AN ANIMAL　　　　　　　　　　　　　　　　NOUN

of _____.
　　　LIQUID

In Science lab, we dissected a _____ and saw its
　　　　　　　　　　　　　　　　　　　　　　NOUN

_____ and _____ . Some people got sick
　　　NOUN　　　　　　　　　　NOUN

and _____ when we did this. Sometimes we would have
　　　VERB (PAST TENSE)

a _____ show. Some of the students would
　　　　　NOUN

_____ to _____ music, while others re-
　　　VERB　　　　　　　　　NOUN

cited _____. The best was when three boys
　　　　NOUN

juggled _____ while turning _____
　　　　　PLURAL NOUN　　　　　　　　　　　PLURAL NOUN

and standing on their _____.
　　　　　　　　　PART OF BODY (PLURAL)

From *Sooper Dooper Mad Libs*® ● Copyright © 1988 Price Stern Sloan, Inc.,
A member of The Putnam & Grosset Group, New York, New York.

MAD LIBS® is fun to play with friends, but you can also play it by yourself!
To begin with, DO NOT look at the story on the page below. Fill in the blanks
on this page with the words called for. Then, using the words you've selected, fill
in the blank spaces in the story.
Now you've created your own hilarious MAD LIB!

THE STOCK MARKET or CAPITALISM MADE EASY

PLURAL NOUN: _____

ADJECTIVE: _____

PLURAL NOUN: _____

ANIMAL: _____

NOUN: _____

ADJECTIVE: _____

ADJECTIVE: _____

PLURAL NOUN: _____

NOUN: _____

ADJECTIVE: _____

NOUN: _____

NOUN: _____

ADJECTIVE: _____

NOUN: _____

PLURAL NOUN: _____

ADJECTIVE: _____

NOUN: _____

THE STOCK MARKET
or CAPITALISM MADE EASY

This is how I made one million _____ in the stock
PLURAL NOUN

market. It's simple. At the present time, any _____
ADJECTIVE

investor with a little capital should be able to double his_____
PLURAL NOUN

in a few months. All the experts agree that we are nearing the end of

the _____ market. Just recently, for instance, the
ANIMAL

American _____ and Foundry Company has shown
NOUN

a/an _____ trend. Conditions indicate a/an _____
ADJECTIVE   ADJECTIVE

market for their principal product, automatic _____.
PLURAL NOUN

International Telephone and _____ Company also
NOUN

looks _____. At the end of the last fiscal _____
ADJECTIVE   NOUN

they were earning $10 a/an _____. Another _____
NOUN   ADJECTIVE

tip is Consolidated _____. This outfit manufactures
NOUN

and sells electronic _____ of a very _____
PLURAL NOUN   ADJECTIVE

quality. But whatever you do, act now. Remember, prosperity is just

around the _____.
NOUN

From *Sooper Dooper Mad Libs*® ● Copyright © 1988 Price Stern Sloan, Inc.,
A member of The Putnam & Grosset Group, New York, New York.

MAD LIBS® is fun to play with friends, but you can also play it by yourself!
To begin with, DO NOT look at the story on the page below. Fill in the blanks
on this page with the words called for. Then, using the words you've selected, fill
in the blank spaces in the story.
Now you've created your own hilarious MAD LIB!

THE PLUMBER'S VISIT

GIRL IN ROOM: _____

BOY IN ROOM: _____

ADVERB: _____

NOUN: _____

NOUN: _____

ADJECTIVE: _____

NOUN: _____

LIQUID: _____

NOUN: _____

EXCLAMATION: _____

ADJECTIVE: _____

NOUN: _____

NOUN: _____

PLURAL NOUN: _____

NOUN: _____

THE PLUMBER'S VISIT

A dramatic scene to be played by _____ and

GIRL IN ROOM

_____

BOY IN ROOM

GIRL: Are you the plumber I sent for?

BOY: Yes, madam. I came over as _____ as I could. Is

ADVERB

there something wrong with your _____?

NOUN

GIRL: No, it's my _____. The _____ thing

NOUN ADJECTIVE

is all stopped up.

BOY: Have you tried cleaning it with a/an _____?

NOUN

GIRL: Yes, but there was too much _____ in the

LIQUID

_____.

NOUN

BOY: _____! This looks like it's going to be a/an

EXCLAMATION

_____ job!

ADJECTIVE

GIRL: Do you think I'll need a new _____?

NOUN

BOY: Well, if your _____ is cracked, I'll have to

NOUN

tighten up your _____. Then I can tell.

PLURAL NOUN

GIRL: All right. But just make sure you don't scratch my

_____.

NOUN

From *Sooper Dooper Mad Libs*® ● Copyright © 1988 Price Stern Sloan, Inc.,
A member of The Putnam & Grosset Group, New York, New York.

MAD LIBS® is fun to play with friends, but you can also play it by yourself!
To begin with, DO NOT look at the story on the page below. Fill in the blanks
on this page with the words called for. Then, using the words you've selected, fill
in the blank spaces in the story.
Now you've created your own hilarious MAD LIB!

PILOT TO PASSENGERS

ADJECTIVE: _____

CELEBRITY: _____

NOUN: _____

ADJECTIVE: _____

GEOGRAPHICAL LOCATION: _____

NUMBER: _____

NUMBER: _____

LIQUID: _____

ADJECTIVE: _____

NOUN: _____

VERB: _____

ADJECTIVE: _____

NOUN: _____

ADJECTIVE: _____

PLURAL NOUN: _____

ADJECTIVE: _____

PILOT TO PASSENGERS

Ladies and gentlemen, welcome aboard _____ Airlines'
                                        ADJECTIVE

Flight 750. This is your captain and pilot, _____. The
                                              CELEBRITY

plane you are traveling on is a DC-10 Strato-_____ with
                                               NOUN

four _____ engines. At present, we are directly over
      ADJECTIVE

_____. Our speed is _____ miles per hour
GEOGRAPHICAL LOCATION   NUMBER

and we are flying at an altitude of_____ feet. If you care
                                    NUMBER

for a cup of_____ or a/an _____ sandwich,
             LIQUID   ADJECTIVE

please push the _____ located over your seat and our
                 NOUN

stewardess will be glad to _____ you. We have a/an
                            VERB

_____ tail wind and will soon be flying through a heavy
  ADJECTIVE

_____ storm. So I'll have to ask you all to fasten your
  NOUN

_____ belts and put your _____ in the ash
  ADJECTIVE   PLURAL NOUN

tray. In the meantime, I hope you have a/an _____ trip.
                                              ADJECTIVE

MAD LIBS® is fun to play with friends, but you can also play it by yourself! To begin with, DO NOT look at the story on the page below. Fill in the blanks on this page with the words called for. Then, using the words you've selected, fill in the blank spaces in the story.
Now you've created your own hilarious MAD LIB!

YUPPIES

NOUN:_____

NUMBER:_____

ADJECTIVE:_____

VERB (PAST TENSE):_____

ADVERB:_____

ADJECTIVE:_____

VERB:_____

ADJECTIVE:_____

ADJECTIVE:_____

NOUN:_____

A LIQUID:_____

ADJECTIVE:_____

ADJECTIVE:_____

NOUN:_____

NOUN:_____

YUPPIES

Yuppies are also called _____ boomers. They were
NOUN

born after World War _____. You can identify them by
NUMBER

their _____ hair, _____ shirts and
ADJECTIVE   VERB (PAST TENSE)

_____ _____ shoes. They are
ADVERB   ADJECTIVE

_____-aholics, make lots of money and have
VERB

_____ taste. They dine at the most
ADJECTIVE

_____ restaurants, eat fresh _____
ADJECTIVE   NOUN

(formerly known as spaghetti) and always order mineral

_____ They all sport glasses, even if they have
A LIQUID

_____ vision. They know a little about everything, and
ADJECTIVE

so tend to have _____ taste. Yuppies are really just
ADJECTIVE

hippies that decided it was better to make _____ not
NOUN

_____.
NOUN

MAD LIBS® is fun to play with friends, but you can also play it by yourself! To begin with, DO NOT look at the story on the page below. Fill in the blanks on this page with the words called for. Then, using the words you've selected, fill in the blank spaces in the story.

Now you've created your own hilarious MAD LIB!

FOOTBALL BROADCAST

ANIMAL (PLURAL): _____

PLURAL NOUN: _____

NOUN: _____

MALE CELEBRITY: _____

NOUN: _____

NOUN: _____

NUMBER: _____

CELEBRITY: _____

ADJECTIVE: _____

CELEBRITY: _____

ADJECTIVE: _____

NOUN: _____

NOUN: _____

VERB ENDING IN "ING": _____

FOOTBALL BROADCAST

Good afternoon, ladies and gentlemen. This is your favorite sportscaster bringing you the big football game between the Columbia University _____ and the West Point _____.
                                                ANIMAL (PLURAL)   PLURAL NOUN

The center has just snapped the _____ back to the
                                 NOUN

Columbia star halfback, _____, who is running
                         MALE CELEBRITY

around his own left _____. There he's tackled hard
                     NOUN

around the _____. Now it's West Point's ball and
            NOUN

_____ to go. They're coming out of the huddle. The ball
  NUMBER

is snapped back to _____, who fades back and throws a
                    CELEBRITY

long, _____ pass which is caught by _____,
       ADJECTIVE   CELEBRITY

who is West Point's _____ quarterback. He's in the
                     ADJECTIVE

clear and he races over the _____ for a touchdown! No,
                             NOUN

no, wait! The referee is calling the play back to the 35 _____
                                                          NOUN

line. He's going to penalize West Point for _____.
                                             VERB ENDING IN "ING"

MAD LIBS® is fun to play with friends, but you can also play it by yourself!
To begin with, DO NOT look at the story on the page below. Fill in the blanks
on this page with the words called for. Then, using the words you've selected, fill
in the blank spaces in the story.
Now you've created your own hilarious MAD LIB!

DESCRIPTION OF A HORROR TV SHOW

AN ANIMAL: _____

A PERSON: _____

AN OCCUPATION: _____

A PERSON: _____

NOUN: _____

A PLACE: _____

A LIQUID: _____

ADJECTIVE: _____

NOUN: _____

ADJECTIVE: _____

NOUN: _____

NOUN: _____

A PERSON: _____

ADVERB: _____

DESCRIPTION OF A HORROR TV SHOW

Last week, I saw a television show that really gave me _____
                                                        AN ANIMAL

pimples! It starred _____ as a mad _____
                        A PERSON   AN OCCUPATION

who discovers a way to make bedbugs fourteen feet high!

The scientist has a goofy assistant, played by _____,
                                                    A PERSON

who gets mad because the scientist keeps hitting him on the head

with a/an _____. So he lets the bedbugs loose. Right
              NOUN

away they start to eat up _____. The army tries to stop
                              A PLACE

them by spraying them with _____ but that doesn't
                                A LIQUID

bother those _____ bedbugs. They go right on and eat
                ADJECTIVE

up Chicago. Then the army drops an atom _____ on
                                            NOUN

them and this kills all of them except one super bedbug who grabs

the _____ scientist and jumps into a volcano. And then
        ADJECTIVE

the goofy assistant takes off his disguise and says, "I was only a/an

_____ for the F.B.I.," and he marries the scientist's
      NOUN

beautiful _____, who is played by _____,
              NOUN   A PERSON

and they live _____ ever after.
                  ADVERB

MAD LIBS® is fun to play with friends, but you can also play it by yourself!
To begin with, DO NOT look at the story on the page below. Fill in the blanks
on this page with the words called for. Then, using the words you've selected, fill
in the blank spaces in the story.
Now you've created your own hilarious MAD LIB!

SUPERSTITIONS

A NUMBER: _____

NOUN: _____

NOUN: _____

NOUN: _____

ADJECTIVE: _____

NOUN: _____

A FOOD: _____

NOUN: _____

ADJECTIVE: _____

NOUN: _____

PLURAL NOUN: _____

NOUN: _____

PLURAL NOUN: _____

NOUN: _____

SUPERSTITIONS

When I was a kid _____ years ago, we used to believe in
            A NUMBER

superstitions like it's bad luck to open a/an _____ in the
                                             NOUN

house, and if your _____ itches, it means a/an _____
                    NOUN   NOUN

is coming to visit, and you'll have _____ luck if you find
                                     ADJECTIVE

a four-leaf-_____. And we believed that if you spilled
            NOUN

_____ at the table, you had to throw some over your,
      A FOOD

left _____, and if your _____ toe
         NOUN   ADJECTIVE

hurt, it meant rain, and if you broke a/an _____
                                            NOUN

you would have seven years of bad _____.
                                   PLURAL NOUN

Today kids have different superstitions such as, it's bad luck to jump

on the railroad tracks just before a/an _____ pulls in,
                                         NOUN

and don't throw _____ at policemen. But, actually,
                  PLURAL NOUN

there's only one superstition I believe in. Whenever I comment on

my health, I always remember to knock on a piece of _____.
                                                      NOUN

MAD LIBS® is fun to play with friends, but you can also play it by yourself!
To begin with, DO NOT look at the story on the page below. Fill in the blanks
on this page with the words called for. Then, using the words you've selected,
fill in the blank spaces in the story.
Now you've created your own hilarious MAD LIB!

THE SECRET AGENT

NUMBER: _____

ADJECTIVE: _____

GEOGRAPHIC LOCATION: _____

ADJECTIVE: _____

PLURAL NOUN: _____

NAME OF GIRL IN ROOM: _____

NOUN: _____

ADJECTIVE: _____

VERB: _____

NOUN: _____

NOUN: _____

NOUN: _____

PLURAL NOUN: _____

A RUSSIAN WORD: _____

EXCLAMATION: _____

THE SECRET AGENT

James Bond, Secret Agent Double-0 _____, was in a

NUMBER

tight spot. He was trapped in the _____ jungle of

ADJECTIVE

_____ and the _____

GEOGRAPHICAL LOCATION   ADJECTIVE

_____ were closing in. He glanced at his companion,

PLURAL NOUN

_____. The expression on her face was full of

NAME OF GIRL IN ROOM

_____. He remembered all their _____

NOUN   ADJECTIVE

times together. He was about to _____ from the

VERB

_____, when he felt a cold _____

NOUN   NOUN

in the small of his _____.

NOUN

"Put up your _____!" his companion said, "I too

PLURAL NOUN

am a spy. My real name in Olga _____."

A RUSSIAN WORD

"_____!" exclaimed Bond. "This will cost me

EXCLAMATION

my Christmas bonus."

MAD LIBS® is fun to play with friends, but you can also play it by yourself!
To begin with, DO NOT look at the story on the page below. Fill in the blanks
on this page with the words called for. Then, using the words you've selected, fill
in the blank spaces in the story.
Now you've created your own hilarious MAD LIB!

REVIEW OF A MONSTER MOVIE

NOUN: _____

ADJECTIVE: _____

MOVIE ACTOR: _____

ADJECTIVE: _____

ADJECTIVE: _____

PLURAL NOUN: _____

PLURAL NOUN: _____

A COLOR: _____

NUMBER: _____

A CELEBRITY: _____

A FEMALE CELEBRITY: _____

A TOWN: _____

MOVIE STAR: _____

ADVERB: _____

REVIEW OF A MONSTER MOVIE

A new movie has just opened called, "The Teen-Age _____
NOUN

Meets the _____ Vampire from Outer Space."
ADJECTIVE

At the opening, we see the teen-age hero, played by _____
MOVIE ACTOR

who is a/an _____ scientist. He is trying to build a/an
ADJECTIVE

_____ monster out of old _____ and used
ADJECTIVE   PLURAL NOUN

_____.
PLURAL NOUN

The monster has _____ skin and _____ arms,
A COLOR   NUMBER

and is played by _____.
A CELEBRITY

Suddenly the monster comes to life and kidnaps the beautiful

heroine, played by _____. Then he begins to destroy
A FEMALE CELEBRITY

_____.
A TOWN

In the end, the monster is destroyed by the vampire who is played by

_____. And the hero and the heroine live _____
MOVIE STAR   ADVERB

ever after.

MAD LIBS® is fun to play with friends, but you can also play it by yourself! To begin with, DO NOT look at the story on the page below. Fill in the blanks on this page with the words called for. Then, using the words you've selected, fill in the blank spaces in the story.

Now you've created your own hilarious MAD LIB!

SCIENCE FICTION STORY

NOUN: _____

GEOGRAPHICAL LOCATION: _____

A NUMBER: _____

ADVERB: _____

A NONSENSE WORD: _____

NOUN: _____

NONSENSE WORD: _____

VERB: _____

NONSENSE WORD: _____

EXCLAMATION: _____

NONSENSE WORD: _____

NONSENSE WORD: _____

NONSENSE WORD: _____

SCIENCE FICTION STORY

Major Zarnak, of the Inter-Galactic Space Patrol, deactivated his

hyper-_____ overdrive and landed his space ship on the
NOUN

planet _____. On leaving the decompression
GEOGRAPHICAL LOCATION

chamber, he saw a/an _____-armed monster
A NUMBER

approaching _____. He shouted, "_____,"
ADVERB   A NONSENSE WORD

the Galactic word for peace, but the monster whipped out a

disintegrator _____ and tried to _____ him.
NOUN   NONSENSE WORD

Major Zarnak ducked and _____ the monster
VERB

with his subsonic _____.
NONSENSE WORD

"_____!" said the monster, clutching his
EXCLAMATION

_____.
NONSENSE WORD

"_____" replied Major Zarnak cleverly, and
NONSENSE WORD

getting back into his space ship, he zipped back to his headquarters

on the planet _____.
NONSENSE WORD

MAD LIBS® is fun to play with friends, but you can also play it by yourself!
To begin with, DO NOT look at the story on the page below. Fill in the blanks
on this page with the words called for. Then, using the words you've selected, fill
in the blank spaces in the story.
Now you've created your own hilarious MAD LIB!

HOW TO DO THAT NEW DANCE,

THE MONSTROSITY

ADVERB: _____

NUMBER: _____

PLURAL NOUN: _____

VERB: _____

PART OF THE BODY: _____

VERB: _____

ADVERB: _____

PLURAL NOUN: _____

PLURAL NOUN: _____

PLURAL NOUN: _____

NONSENSE WORD: _____

VERB: _____

NUMBER: _____

VERB: _____

HOW TO DO THAT NEW DANCE, THE MONSTROSITY

(Two brave volunteers are needed to follow the instructions as they are read):

Here's how you do the Monstrosity. First, stand with your feet together. Now move your left foot _____ to the side.
ADVERB

Now stamp your right foot _____ times and put your
NUMBER

hands on your partner's _____. Next, you both
PLURAL NOUN

_____ slowly to the right and bend your _____
VERB   PART OF THE BODY

backward. Now for the next eight counts, both of you _____
VERB

_____ to the left. Next, you and your partner stand back
ADVERB

to back and wiggle your _____ and slap your _____
PLURAL NOUN   PLURAL NOUN

together. Don't forget to keep stamping your right foot. Now face

your partner again, put your _____ together and
PLURAL NOUN

shout, "_____!" Now _____ backward
NONSENSE WORD   VERB

and repeat the whole thing _____ times. If you feel that
NUMBER

you can't learn this dance, you can always _____ the
VERB

the next one out.

MAD LIBS® is fun to play with friends, but you can also play it by yourself!
To begin with, DO NOT look at the story on the page below. Fill in the blanks
on this page with the words called for. Then, using the words you've selected, fill
in the blank spaces in the story.
Now you've created your own hilarious MAD LIB!

AUDITION LETTER FOR TALENT SEARCH

NAME OF TV PERSONALITY: _____

NUMBER: _____

ADJECTIVE: _____

NOUN: _____

NOUN: _____

NOUN: _____

PLURAL NOUN: _____

ADJECTIVE: _____

NOUN: _____

NOUN: _____

A PERSON: _____

A PERSON: _____

NOUN: _____

A PERSON IN ROOM: _____

AUDITION LETTER FOR TALENT SEARCH

Dear _____:
         NAME OF TV PERSONALITY

I am _____ years old, and I would like to audition for
       NUMBER

the talent search you're having on your _____ television
                      ADJECTIVE

program. You are my favorite TV _____ and I think you
                      NOUN

would like my act. I open by playing the _____. Then I
                      NOUN

sing "Somewhere Over the _____" while juggling three
              NOUN

_____. Then for a really _____ finish to my
  PLURAL NOUN   ADJECTIVE

act, I recite Lincoln's Gettysburg _____ and go off stage
                  NOUN

waving an American _____. If you give me the chance, I'm
         NOUN

sure that I can become another _____ or maybe
                  A PERSON

even another _____. And when I become rich
         A PERSON

and famous, I'll always tell everyone that you gave me my first big

_____.
  NOUN

Yours Truly,

_____
A PERSON IN ROOM

MAD LIBS® is fun to play with friends, but you can also play it by yourself!
To begin with, DO NOT look at the story on the page below. Fill in the blanks
on this page with the words called for. Then, using the words you've selected, fill
in the blank spaces in the story.
Now you've created your own hilarious MAD LIB!

DIALOGUE BETWEEN A HILLBILLY

HUSBAND AND WIFE

(VERY DRAMATIC)

VERB: _____

PLURAL NOUN: _____

REPEAT SAME PLURAL NOUN: _____

REPEAT SAME PLURAL NOUN: _____

AN ANIMAL: _____

PLURAL NOUN: _____

AN ANIMAL: _____

VERB: _____

A LIQUID: _____

A FOOD: _____

NOUN: _____

DIALOGUE BETWEEN A HILLBILLY
HUSBAND AND WIFE

(VERY DRAMATIC)

MAW: Paw, git up. It's time to _____ the hogs and milk
$\quad$ VERB

the _____.
$\quad$ PLURAL NOUN

PAW: Milk the _____? Listen, I milked them
$\quad$ REPEAT SAME PL. NOUN

_____ last night.
$\quad$ REPEAT SAME PL. NOUN

MAW: Well, git up. Listen, the old red _____ is
$\quad$ AN ANIMAL

crowing.

PAW: What's fer breakfast? Corn pone and black-eyed _____?
$\quad$ PL. NOUN

MAW: No. I got some nice fried _____ belly.
$\quad$ AN ANIMAL

PAW: Good. After breakfast, I'll _____ the chickens
$\quad$ VERB

and then I'll have to fix the still.

MAW: What's wrong with the still?

PAW: It's turning out _____ instead of moonshine. I
$\quad$ A LIQUID

think I've been putting too much _____ in the
$\quad$ A FOOD

mash.

MAW: Well, don't forget to take your rifle, Paw. If a Revenue

Agent spots you, you can shoot him in the _____.
$\quad$ NOUN

MAD LIBS® is fun to play with friends, but you can also play it by yourself! To begin with, DO NOT look at the story on the page below. Fill in the blanks on this page with the words called for. Then, using the words you've selected, fill in the blank spaces in the story.
Now you've created your own hilarious MAD LIB!

MADISON AVENUE MAD LIBS

ADJECTIVE: _____

NOUN: _____

NOUN: _____

VERB: _____

ADJECTIVE: _____

NOUN: _____

VERB ENDING IN "ING": _____

ADVERB: _____

NOUN: _____

NOUN: _____

PLURAL NOUN: _____

NOUN: _____

PLURAL NOUN: _____

VERB: _____

ADJECTIVE: _____

ANIMAL: _____

PLURAL NOUN: _____

PLURAL NOUN: _____

NUMBER: _____

NOUN: _____

PLURAL NOUN: _____

NOUN: _____

PLURAL NOUN: _____

MADISON AVENUE MAD LIBS

1. _____ _____ don't leave
   ADJECTIVE   NOUN

   _____ without it.
   NOUN

2. When you _____ enough to send the very
                      VERB

   _____.
   ADJECTIVE

3. It's such a pleasure to take the _____ and leave the
                                              NOUN

   _____to us.
   VERB ENDING IN "ING"

4. Drive _____. The _____ you save may
              ADVERB   NOUN

   be your own.

5. Is it live or is it _____?
                                NOUN

6. Four out of five _____ recommend _____
                           PLURAL NOUN   NOUN

   for their _____ who _____ gum.
                    PLURAL NOUN   VERB

7. _____, the _____ says, "Only
        ADJECTIVE   ANIMAL

   you can prevent forest _____."
                                    PLURAL NOUN

8. _____, no one can eat just _____.
        PLURAL NOUN   NUMBER

9. Things go better with _____.
                                  NOUN

10. _____ melt in your _____,
         PLURAL NOUN   NOUN

    not in your_____.
                        PLURAL NOUN

MAD LIBS® is fun to play with friends, but you can also play it by yourself!
To begin with, DO NOT look at the story on the page below. Fill in the blanks
on this page with the words called for. Then, using the words you've selected, fill
in the blank spaces in the story.
Now you've created your own hilarious MAD LIB!

A CHRISTMAS POEM

NOUN: _____

NOUN: _____

PLURAL NOUN: _____

PLURAL NOUN: _____

ADJECTIVE: _____

NOUN: _____

NOUN: _____

ADJECTIVE: _____

PLURAL NOUN: _____

PLURAL NOUN: _____

NOUN: _____

NOUN: _____

VERB PAST TENSE: _____

ADJECTIVE: _____

A CHRISTMAS POEM

'Twas the night before Christmas and all thru the _____

NOUN

Not a creature was stirring, not even a/an _____.

NOUN

The _____ were tucked, all snug in their

PLURAL NOUN

_____,

PLURAL NOUN

While visions of _____ plums danced in their heads.

ADJECTIVE

Then up on the _____ there arose such a clatter,

NOUN

I sprang from my _____ to see what was the matter.

NOUN

It was St. Nicholas with his little _____ belly

ADJECTIVE

That shook when he laughed like a bowl full of _____.

PLURAL NOUN

He spoke not a word, but went straight to his work

And filled all the _____, then turned with a jerk,

PLURAL NOUN

And laying his _____ aside of his nose,

NOUN

And giving a nod, up the _____ he rose.

NOUN

And I heard him exclaim as he _____ out of sight,

VERB PAST TENSE

_____ Christmas to all, and to all a good night!

ADJECTIVE

MAD LIBS® is fun to play with friends, but you can also play it by yourself!
To begin with, DO NOT look at the story on the page below. Fill in the blanks
on this page with the words called for. Then, using the words you've selected, fill
in the blank spaces in the story.
Now you've created your own hilarious MAD LIB!

DESCRIPTION OF A PRIZE FIGHT

PLURAL NOUN: _____

A FAMOUS BUILDING: _____

ADJECTIVE: _____

NAME OF PERSON IN ROOM: _____

ADJECTIVE: _____

NAME OF PERSON IN ROOM: _____

NUMBER: _____

ADVERB: _____

ADJECTIVE: _____

NOUN: _____

NOUN: _____

NOUN: _____

NOUN: _____

ADVERB: _____

EXCLAMATION: _____

ADJECTIVE: _____

DESCRIPTION OF A PRIZE FIGHT

Good evening, sports _____. I'm speaking to you from
PLURAL NOUN

the ringside at the famous _____ and bringing you a
A FAMOUS BUILDING

blow-by-blow description of the _____ fight between
ADJECTIVE

Rocky _____ and the _____ champion,
NAME OF PERSON IN ROOM   ADJECTIVE

Slugger _____. As the bell rings for round _____,
NAME OF PERSON IN ROOM   NUMBER

Rocky moves _____ to the center of the ring and throws
ADVERB

a/an _____ right to Slugger's _____. But
ADJECTIVE   NOUN

Slugger blocks the punch with his _____ and hits Rocky
NOUN

right on the _____ with a tremendous uppercut that
NOUN

knocks him flat on his _____. The referee is counting
NOUN

and the fans are cheering _____. _____!
ADVERB   EXCLAMATION

What a/an _____fight this has been!
ADJECTIVE

From *Monster Mad Libs*® ● Copyright © 1965, 1982, 1988 Price Stern Sloan, Inc.,
A member of The Putnam & Grosset Group, New York, New York.

MAD LIBS® is fun to play with friends, but you can also play it by yourself!
To begin with, DO NOT look at the story on the page below. Fill in the blanks
on this page with the words called for. Then, using the words you've selected,
fill in the blank spaces in the story.
Now you've created your own hilarious MAD LIB!

A ONE ACT SURVEY

NAME OF MAN IN ROOM: _____

VERB ENDING IN "ING": _____

NOUN: _____

NUMBER:: _____

ADJECTIVE: _____

NOUN: _____

NOUN: _____

ADJECTIVE: _____

NOUN: _____

VERB: _____

NOUN: _____

NOUN: _____

NOUN: _____

NOUN: _____

NUMBER: _____

NOUN: _____

NOUN: _____

ADJECTIVE: _____

PLURAL NOUN: _____

PLURAL NOUN: _____

A ONE ACT SURVEY

MAN: Good day, Madame. My name is _____,
NAME OF MAN IN ROOM

and I'd like to ask you a few questions about your career

in _____. Tell me, how many years have
VERB ENDING IN "ING"

you been working in the _____ field?
NOUN

WOMAN: About _____ years, sometimes it feels
NUMBER

like more when I've had a _____ day.
ADJECTIVE

MAN: Do you find it hard being a _____
NOUN

in the business _____?
NOUN

WOMAN: Yes, I think it's _____.
ADJECTIVE

MAN: Do you have a _____ degree? And, if so,
NOUN

from what University did you _____?
VERB

WOMAN: I received my Bachelor of _____ and my Masters
NOUN

of _____ from the University of _____.
NOUN   NOUN

MAN: How much _____ do you make?
NOUN

WOMAN: I make _____ a year plus benifits like
NUMBER

_____ insurance and _____ insurance.
NOUN   NOUN

MAN: I appreciate your _____ cooperation. I wish
ADJECTIVE

I had your job. Do they need any more _____?
PLURAL NOUN

WOMAN: No, we have enough _____ at the office, thank you.
PLURAL NOUN

MAD LIBS ® is fun to play with friends, but you can also play it by yourself!
To begin with, DO NOT look at the story on the page below. Fill in the blanks
on this page with the words called for. Then, using the words you've selected, fill
in the blank spaces in the story.
Now you've created your own hilarious MAD LIB!

WHY YOU SHOULD GO TO COLLEGE

ADJECTIVE: _____

PLURAL NOUN: _____

PLURAL NOUN: _____

PLURAL NOUN: _____

ADJECTIVE: _____

ADJECTIVE: _____

PLURAL NOUN: _____

NUMBER: _____

NOUN: _____

PLURAL NOUN: _____

AN OCCUPATION: _____

AN OCCUPATION: _____

PLURAL NOUN: _____

ADJECTIVE: _____

WHY YOU SHOULD GO TO COLLEGE

Our American universities offer students many _____
ADJECTIVE

courses that will prepare them to become good _____.
PLURAL NOUN

You can get a degree as a Bachelor of _____, or take a
PLURAL NOUN

regular liberal _____ course. Or, if you want to become
PLURAL NOUN

a/an _____ engineer, you can study _____
ADJECTIVE   ADJECTIVE

mathematics and differential _____. Then after
PLURAL NOUN

_____ years, if you want to continue your studies, you
NUMBER

can write a/an _____ and become a Doctor of_____.
NOUN   PLURAL NOUN

When you get out into the world, if you have a diploma from a

university, you will be able to get a job as a/an _____. If
AN OCCUPATION

you don't have a diploma, you will have to take a job as a/an

_____. So it's important that you study hard in
AN OCCUPATION

high school so you will do well on your College Entrance_____.
PLURAL NOUN

Remember, "A little learning is a/an _____ thing."
ADJECTIVE

MAD LIBS® is fun to play with friends, but you can also play it by yourself! To begin with, DO NOT look at the story on the page below. Fill in the blanks on this page with the words called for. Then, using the words you've selected, fill in the blank spaces in the story.

Now you've created your own hilarious MAD LIB!

FINAL EXAM

ADJECTIVE: _____

A PERSON: _____

NOUN: _____

PLURAL NOUN: _____

NOUN: _____

NOUN: _____

A PERSON: _____

NUMBER: _____

PLURAL NOUN: _____

NOUN: _____

PLURAL NOUN: _____

FINAL EXAM

Well, it's time for final exams again. Here are some sample

questions with _____ answers that may give you an idea
                  ADJECTIVE

what final exams are like:

QUESTION: Who was the first president of the United States?

ANSWER: _____, who was also called, "The
            A PERSON

          _____ of Our Country."
              NOUN

QUESTION: What is the shortest distance between two

          _____?
            PLURAL NOUN

ANSWER: A straight _____.
                          NOUN

QUESTION: Who said, "I regret that I only have one _____
                                                      NOUN

          to give for my country."?

ANSWER: _____.
            A PERSON

QUESTION: If two apples cost _____ cents and ten
                                NUMBER

          _____ cost fifty cents, how much would
            PLURAL NOUN

          one _____ cost?
                  NOUN

ANSWER: What are you? Some kind of a nut or something? If

          you answer questions like these, you should end up

          with the best _____ in class.
                           PLURAL NOUN

MAD LIBS® is fun to play with friends, but you can also play it by yourself!
To begin with, DO NOT look at the story on the page below. Fill in the blanks
on this page with the words called for. Then, using the words you've selected, fill
in the blank spaces in the story.
Now you've created your own hilarious MAD LIB!

THE ASTRONAUT

A MALE CELEBRITY: _____

A MALE CELEBRITY: _____

A NUMBER: _____

PLURAL NOUN: _____

ADJECTIVE: _____

PLURAL NOUN: _____

ADJECTIVE: _____

NOUN: _____

GEOGRAPHICAL LOCATION: _____

A PLACE: _____

PLURAL NOUN: _____

PLURAL NOUN: _____

THE ASTRONAUT

As everyone knows, the first U.S. man to go into space was

_____. Many astronauts have travelled in
     A MALE CELEBRITY

space since. One of the next spacemen will be _____. He
                                       A MALE CELEBRITY

will reach an altitude of _____ feet in only 15
                              A NUMBER

seconds. Then, he will fire his second-stage _____ and
                                    PLURAL NOUN

go into a/an _____ orbit. At this point, the electronic
           ADJECTIVE

equipment will start sending _____ back to earth. After
                        PLURAL NOUN

1000 trips around the earth, his _____ vehicle will re-
                         ADJECTIVE

enter the _____ and come down over _____,
         NOUN   GEOGRAPHICAL LOCATION

and he will fly it to _____. After that, a team of
                  A PLACE

_____ and _____ will visit the moon again.
  PLURAL NOUN   PLURAL NOUN

MAD LIBS® is fun to play with friends, but you can also play it by yourself!
To begin with, DO NOT look at the story on the page below. Fill in the blanks
on this page with the words called for. Then, using the words you've selected, fill
in the blank spaces in the story.
Now you've created your own hilarious MAD LIB!

YOU HAVE WRITTEN A

NUCLEAR TEST BAN TREATY

A PLACE: _____

PLURAL NOUN: _____

PLURAL NOUN: _____

PLURAL NOUN: _____

ADVERB: _____

NOUN: _____

YOU HAVE WRITTEN A NEW LAW

NOUN (REPEAT NEXT 3 SPACES): _____

SAME NOUN: _____

SAME NOUN: _____

SAME NOUN: _____

A PLACE: _____

NUMBER: _____

A LIQUID: _____

YOU HAVE WRITTEN A
NUCLEAR TEST BAN TREATY

It is hereby agreed by the Big Three, The United States, Russia, and

_____, that there will be no further testing of nuclear
    A PLACE

_____. However, tests may be made under _____.
  PLURAL NOUN   PLURAL NOUN

Explosions must be limited to one-half megaton, which is equal to

500,000 tons of _____. We all agree that this sounds
                    PLURAL NOUN

_____ and is the only way to keep someone from
    ADVERB

blowing up the _____.
                    NOUN

YOU HAVE WRITTEN A NEW LAW

It will be unlawful to own a/an _____ or carry
                                 NOUN (REPEAT NEXT 3 SPACES)

a concealed _____ without a/an _____ license.
              SAME NOUN   SAME NOUN

The penalty for _____-carrying will be thirty days in the
                   SAME NOUN

_____ or a fine of _____ dollars. The
    A PLACE   NUMBER

penalty is double if the person is arrested while under the influence

of _____.
      A LIQUID

MAD LIBS® is fun to play with friends, but you can also play it by yourself! To begin with, DO NOT look at the story on the page below. Fill in the blanks on this page with the words called for. Then, using the words you've selected, fill in the blank spaces in the story.
Now you've created your own hilarious MAD LIB!

SAMPSON AND DELILAH

ADJECTIVE: _____

PLURAL NOUN: _____

NOUN: _____

ADJECTIVE: _____

NOUN: _____

NOUN: _____

DEROGATORY EXCLAMATION: _____

ADJECTIVE: _____

VERB: _____

NOUN: _____

ADJECTIVE: _____

NOUN: _____

ADJECTIVE: _____

SAMPSON AND DELILAH
(A Tragic Dialogue)

DELILAH: Sam Sampson! Will you stop doing those _____
ADJECTIVE

exercises.

SAMPSON: Listen, Delilah. I have to keep my _____
PLURAL NOUN

in shape. After all, I'm the strongest _____
NOUN

in the tribe.

DELILAH: Well, you look _____. Look at the way
ADJECTIVE

your hair hangs down over your _____.
NOUN

SAMPSON: I've been busy. Yesterday I had to kill 10,000 Philis-

tines with the jawbone of a/an _____.
NOUN

DELILAH: _____! You promised to take
DEROGATORY EXCLAMATION

me to a/an _____ party tonight.
ADJECTIVE

SAMPSON: Okay. So I'll _____ my hair.
VERB

DELILAH: I'll do it for you. Now just sit here on this _____,
NOUN

and I'll give you a/an _____ haircut.
ADJECTIVE

SAMPSON: Okay.

DELILAH: There. Your _____ is nice and short.
NOUN

How do you feel?

SAMPSON: _____.
ADJECTIVE

MAD LIBS® is fun to play with friends, but you can also play it by yourself!
To begin with, DO NOT look at the story on the page below. Fill in the blanks
on this page with the words called for. Then, using the words you've selected, fill
in the blank spaces in the story.
Now you've created your own hilarious MAD LIB!

THE GETTYSBURG ADDRESS

PLURAL NOUN: _____

NOUN: _____

ADJECTIVE: _____

PLURAL NOUN: _____

ADJECTIVE: _____

NOUN: _____

SAME NOUN: _____

ADJECTIVE: _____

FAMOUS PERSON: _____

PLURAL NOUN: _____

SAME PLURAL NOUN: _____

SAME PLURAL NOUN: _____

NOUN: _____

THE GETTYSBURG ADDRESS

Four score and seven years ago, our _____ brought
                                        PLURAL NOUN

forth on this _____ a/an _____ nation
                    NOUN   ADJECTIVE

conceived in liberty and dedicated to the proposition that all

_____ are created _____. Now we are en-
   PLURAL NOUN   ADJECTIVE

gaged in a great civil war, testing whether that _____ or
                                                      NOUN

any _____ so conceived and so dedicated can long
        SAME NOUN

endure. It is rather for us to be here dedicated to the _____
                                                           ADJECTIVE

task remaining before us . . . so that this nation under _____
                                                            FAMOUS PERSON

shall have a new birth of freedom, and that government of the

_____, by the _____, and for the
   PLURAL NOUN   SAME PLURAL NOUN

_____ shall not perish from the _____.
   SAME PLURAL NOUN   NOUN

MAD LIBS® is fun to play with friends, but you can also play it by yourself!
To begin with, DO NOT look at the story on the page below. Fill in the blanks
on this page with the words called for. Then, using the words you've selected, fill
in the blank spaces in the story.
Now you've created your own hilarious MAD LIB!

RELATIVES

ADJECTIVE: _____

ADJECTIVE: _____

NOUN: _____

NOUN: _____

NOUN: _____

PLURAL NOUN: _____

PART OF THE BODY: _____

PLURAL NOUN: _____

A FOOD: _____

NOUN: _____

A HOLIDAY: _____

A BIRD: _____

RELATIVES

This is a/an _____ explanation of what relatives are. If
ADJECTIVE

you don't know, you are probably _____. Parents
ADJECTIVE

consist of one mother and one _____. Mothers are
NOUN

always saying "Go comb your_____", or"Stop picking
NOUN

your _____!" Brothers and sisters are called
NOUN

_____and they are often a pain in the_____.
PLURAL NOUN   PART OF THE BODY

Grandfathers and grandmothers are your parents'_____.
PLURAL NOUN

They will buy you _____ when mother says you can't
A FOOD

have any. An aunt is someone who is married to your_____.
NOUN

Relatives only get together on Thanksgiving or_____to
A HOLIDAY

eat a big_____. Do we really need relatives? I doubt it.
A BIRD

MAD LIBS® is fun to play with friends, but you can also play it by yourself!
To begin with, DO NOT look at the story on the page below. Fill in the blanks
on this page with the words called for. Then, using the words you've selected, fill
in the blank spaces in the story.
Now you've created your own hilarious MAD LIB!

MARK ANTHONY'S ADDRESS

FROM 'JULIUS CAESAR'

PLURAL NOUN: _____

PLURAL NOUN: _____

VERB: _____

NAME: _____

NAME: _____

ADJECTIVE: _____

PLURAL NOUN: _____

NOUN: _____

NOUN: _____

NOUN: _____

NOUN: _____

NOUN: _____

PLURAL NOUN: _____

NOUN: _____

MARK ANTHONY'S ADDRESS
FROM 'JULIUS CAESAR'

Friends, Romans, _____, lend me your _____;
PLURAL NOUN   PLURAL NOUN

I come to _____ Caesar, not to praise him. The evil that
VERB

men do lives after them, the good is oft interred with their

_____; so let it be with _____. The noble
NAME   NAME

Brutus hath told you Caesar was _____; if it were so, it
ADJECTIVE

was a grievous fault. If you have _____, prepare to shed
PLURAL NOUN

them now. You all do know this _____. I remember the
NOUN

first time Caesar put it on. Through this the well-beloved Brutus

stabb'd; for Brutus, as you know, was Caesar's _____:
NOUN

this was the unkindest _____ of all. Here is the
NOUN

_____, and under Caesar's seal. To every Roman
NOUN

_____ he gives, to every several man, seventy-five
NOUN

_____. Here was a/an _____!
PLURAL NOUN   NOUN

when comes such another?

From *Monster Mad Libs*® ● Copyright © 1965, 1982, 1988 Price Stern Sloan, Inc.,
A member of The Putnam & Grosset Group, New York, New York.

MAD LIBS® is fun to play with friends, but you can also play it by yourself! To begin with, DO NOT look at the story on the page below. Fill in the blanks on this page with the words called for. Then, using the words you've selected, fill in the blank spaces in the story.
Now you've created your own hilarious MAD LIB!

COLUMBUS AND ISABELLA

A PLACE: _____

PLURAL NOUN: _____

PLURAL NOUN: _____

ADJECTIVE: _____

PLURAL NOUN: _____

NOUN: _____

EXCLAMATION: _____

A PERSON: _____

PLURAL NOUN: _____

A LIQUID: _____

PLURAL NOUN: _____

ADJECTIVE: _____

NOUN: _____

COLUMBUS AND ISABELLA

(Dramatic Scene)

COLUMBUS: Queen Isabella, it is I, Christopher Columbus. I have returned after discovering a new route to

_____.
A PLACE

ISABELLA: That's news, Columbus. Did you bring back lots of

silver and precious _____?
PLURAL NOUN

COLUMBUS: No, your majesty. But you'll never have to pawn the

royal _____ again. I discovered a/an
PLURAL NOUN

_____ land populated by fierce, red
ADJECTIVE

_____, and I claimed them all in the
PLURAL NOUN

name of the Spanish _____.
NOUN

ISABELLA: _____! This will please my husband,
EXCLAMATION

_____. What are these natives called?
A PERSON

COLUMBUS: They are called _____ your majesty.
PLURAL NOUN

They put_____ on their faces and wear
A LIQUID

_____ in their hair.
PLURAL NOUN

ISABELLA: You have made a/an _____ voyage,
ADJECTIVE

Columbus, and your _____ will go
NOUN

down in history!

MAD LIBS®

World's Greatest Word Game

A super silly way to fill in the _____!
(plural noun)

by Roger Price & Leonard Stern

MAD LIBS® is fun to play with friends, but you can also play it by yourself!

To begin with, DO NOT look at the story on the page below. Fill in the blanks on this page with the words called for. Then, using the words you've selected, fill in the blank spaces in the story. Now you've created your own hilarious MAD LIB!

AMUSEMENT PARKS

NOUN: _____

NOUN: _____

ADJECTIVE: _____

NOUN: _____

PLURAL NOUN: _____

NOUN: _____

ADJECTIVE: _____

LIQUID: _____

NOUN: _____

PLURAL NOUN: _____

PLURAL NOUN: _____

NOUN: _____

NOUN: _____

AMUSEMENT PARKS

An amusement park is always fun to visit on a hot summer

_____. When you get there, you can rent a/an
       NOUN

_____ and go for a swim. And there are lots of
   NOUN

_____ things to eat. You can start off with a hot dog on
  ADJECTIVE

a/an_____ with mustard, relish, and_____
    NOUN   PLURAL NOUN

on it. Then you can have a buttered ear of _____ with a
                                   NOUN

nice _____ slice of watermelon and a big bottle of
    ADJECTIVE

cold_____. When you are full, it's time to go on the
   LIQUID

roller coaster, which should settle your _____.
                                NOUN

Other amusement park rides are the Dodge-Em which has little

_____, that you drive and run into other_____,
PLURAL NOUN   PLURAL NOUN

and the Merry-Go-Round where you can sit on a big _____
                                   NOUN

and try to grab the gold _____ as you ride past.
                     NOUN

MAD LIBS® is fun to play with friends, but you can also play it by yourself!
To begin with, DO NOT look at the story on the page below. Fill in the blanks
on this page with the words called for. Then, using the words you've selected, fill
in the blank spaces in the story.
Now you've created your own hilarious MAD LIB!

BULL FIGHTING

ADJECTIVE: _____

GEOGRAPHICAL LOCATION: _____

NOUN: _____

SPANISH WORD: _____

NOUN: _____

ADJECTIVE: _____

ADJECTIVE: _____

PLURAL NOUN: _____

SPANISH WORD: _____

PLURAL NOUN: _____

EXCLAMATION: _____

ADJECTIVE: _____

PLURAL NOUN: _____

BULL FIGHTING

Bullfighting is a/an _____ sport which is very popular
ADJECTIVE

in _____. A bullfighter is called a matador,
GEOGRAPHICAL LOCATION

and his equipment consists of long, sharp _____ called
NOUN

a/an "_____," and a bright red _____.
SPANISH WORD   NOUN

He waves his cape at the bull, which makes the bull _____
ADJECTIVE

and causes him to charge. The matador then goes through a series of

_____ maneuvers to avoid getting caught on the bull's
ADJECTIVE

_____.
PLURAL NOUN

If the matador kills the bull, the spectators yell "_____!"
SPANISH WORD

and throw their _____ into the ring. If the bull wins,
PLURAL NOUN

they yell, "_____!" and call for another matador.
EXCLAMATION

Bullfighting is a very _____ sport, but it will never be
ADJECTIVE

popular in America because Americans don't believe in cruelty to

_____.
PLURAL NOUN

MAD LIBS® is fun to play with friends, but you can also play it by yourself! To begin with, DO NOT look at the story on the page below. Fill in the blanks on this page with the words called for. Then, using the words you've selected, fill in the blank spaces in the story.
Now you've created your own hilarious MAD LIB!

BOWLING

NOUN: _____

ADJECTIVE: _____

PLURAL NOUN: _____

ADJECTIVE: _____

NOUN: _____

NUMBER: _____

A FUNNY NOISE: _____

A FUNNIER NOISE: _____

NOUN: _____

PLURAL NOUN: _____

NOUN: _____

NOUN: _____

NOUN: _____

"BOWLING"

Almost every community in America now has a bowling _____
NOUN

because bowling has become very _____ with young
ADJECTIVE

_____. Many of them become very _____ at
PLURAL NOUN   ADJECTIVE

the game.

The object of the game is to roll a heavy bowling _____
NOUN

down the alley and knock down the _____ pins which
NUMBER

are at the other end. If you knock them down in one roll, it's called

a/an "_____." If it takes two rolls, it's called a/an
A FUNNY NOISE

"_____."
A FUNNIER NOISE

Many alleys have automatic _____ setters. Others hire
NOUN

_____ who set the pins by _____. The most
PLURAL NOUN   NOUN

important thing to remember when bowling is to make sure you

have a good grip on the _____ or you're liable to drop it
NOUN

on your _____. This hurts like anything!
NOUN

MAD LIBS® is fun to play with friends, but you can also play it by yourself!
To begin with, DO NOT look at the story on the page below. Fill in the blanks
on this page with the words called for. Then, using the words you've selected, fill
in the blank spaces in the story.
Now you've created your own hilarious MAD LIB!

A VISIT TO THE ZOO

PLURAL NOUN: _____

PLURAL NOUN: _____

ADJECTIVE: _____

A LIQUID: _____

AN ANIMAL (PLURAL): _____

ADJECTIVE: _____

A FUNNY NOISE: _____

ANOTHER FUNNY NOISE: _____

ADJECTIVE: _____

PLURAL NOUN: _____

NOUN: _____

AN ANIMAL: _____

NOUN: _____

PLURAL NOUN: _____

ADJECTIVE: _____

A VISIT TO THE ZOO

Zoos are places where wild _____ are kept in pens or
PLURAL NOUN

cages so that _____ can come and look at them on
PLURAL NOUN

Sunday afternoons. There are two zoos in New York, one in the

Bronx and one in _____ Park. The Park zoo is built
ADJECTIVE

around a large pond filled with clear sparkling _____.
A LIQUID

Swimming in the pond and eating fish you will see several

_____. When it is feeding time, all of the animals make
AN ANIMAL (PLURAL)

_____ noises. The elephant goes _____
ADJECTIVE   A FUNNY NOISE

and the turtledoves go _____. In one part of the
ANOTHER FUNNY NOISE

zoo, there are two _____ gorillas who love to eat
ADJECTIVE

_____. In another building, there is a spotted African
PLURAL NOUN

_____ that is so fast it can outrun a/an _____.
NOUN   AN ANIMAL

But my favorite animal is the hippopotamus. It has a huge _____
NOUN

and eats fifty pounds of _____ a day. You would never
PLURAL NOUN

know that, technically, it's nothing but an oversized _____
ADJECTIVE

pig.

MAD LIBS® is fun to play with friends, but you can also play it by yourself! To begin with, DO NOT look at the story on the page below. Fill in the blanks on this page with the words called for. Then, using the words you've selected, fill in the blank spaces in the story.

Now you've created your own hilarious MAD LIB!

LITTLE LEAGUE BASEBALL

PLURAL NOUN: _____

PLURAL NOUN: _____

NUMBER: _____

NUMBER: _____

NOUN: _____

ADJECTIVE: _____

PLURAL NOUN: _____

ADJECTIVE: _____

ADJECTIVE: _____

NOUN: _____

NOUN: _____

PLURAL NOUN: _____

PLURAL NOUN: _____

A PERSON: _____

LITTLE LEAGUE BASEBALL

Many future Big League baseball _____ are being

PLURAL NOUN

trained in Little League today. The Little Leagues are just like the

Big League _____ except that players are all between

PLURAL NOUN

_____ and _____ years old.

NUMBER   NUMBER

When a/an _____ goes out for a Little League team, he

NOUN

is given _____ tests in fielding fast _____

ADJECTIVE   PLURAL NOUN

and in hitting. He can either play in the _____ field or in

ADJECTIVE

the _____ field. Or if he has a good throwing _____,

ADJECTIVE   NOUN

he can be a pitcher or catcher. If he can't do anything, he can sit on

the _____. But no matter what position he plays, a Little

NOUN

Leaguer learns to work with his fellow _____ and he

PLURAL NOUN

develops good coordination and strong _____. If you

PLURAL NOUN

play with a Little League team, who knows, you may become a

famous Big League baseball player like _____.

A PERSON

From *Goofy Mad Libs*® ● Copyright © 1988 Price Stern Sloan, Inc.,
A member of The Putnam & Grosset Group, New York, New York.

MAD LIBS® is fun to play with friends, but you can also play it by yourself! To begin with, DO NOT look at the story on the page below. Fill in the blanks on this page with the words called for. Then, using the words you've selected, fill in the blank spaces in the story.
Now you've created your own hilarious MAD LIB!

CONCERT PROGRAM

NAME OF PERSON: _____

PLURAL NOUN: _____

NOUN: _____

NAME OF CITY: _____

NOUN: _____

ADJECTIVE: _____

NOUN: _____

ADJECTIVE: _____

NOUN: _____

MUSICAL INSTRUMENT: _____

NUMBER: _____

ITALIAN WORD: _____

ITALIAN WORD: _____

NOUN: _____

A PLACE: _____

CONCERT PROGRAM

This evening the famous orchestra conductor, _____,

NAME OF PERSON

will present a program of classical _____ at Carnegie

PLURAL NOUN

_____. He will conduct the _____ Sym-

NOUN   NAME OF CITY

phony Orchestra which was formed in 1935. It is noted for its

excellent string and _____-wind sections, considered to

NOUN

be the world's most _____.

ADJECTIVE

The program will begin with Debussy's "Clair de _____,"

NOUN

followed by Mendelssohn's "_____ Song" and Strauss's

ADJECTIVE

"Tales of the Vienna _____." Then we will hear Rach-

NOUN

maninoff's _____ Concerto, Number _____,

MUSICAL INSTRUMENT   NUMBER

but only the _____ and the _____ move-

ITALIAN WORD   ITALIAN WORD

ments. After intermission, the second half of the program will be

devoted to a playing in its entirety of Beethoven's "Fifth

_____." Tickets are on sale at _____.

NOUN   A PLACE

MAD LIBS® is fun to play with friends, but you can also play it by yourself! To begin with, DO NOT look at the story on the page below. Fill in the blanks on this page with the words called for. Then, using the words you've selected, fill in the blank spaces in the story.
Now you've created your own hilarious MAD LIB!

CONTEST

NOUN:_____

ADJECTIVE:_____

ADJECTIVE:_____

NUMBER:_____

NAME OF PERSON IN ROOM:_____

NOUN:_____

ADVERB:_____

NOUN:_____

A FOOD:_____

NOUN:_____

NOUN:_____

PLURAL NOUN:_____

NOUN:_____

PLURAL NOUN:_____

PLURAL NOUN:_____

CONTEST

A gigantic contest in which you already may be a/an

_____. Anyone, and we mean anyone, can enter
NOUN

this _____ contest. Just follow these
ADJECTIVE

_____ rules. Write down in _____
ADJECTIVE   NUMBER

words or less why you think _____ should be
NAME OF PERSON IN ROOM

elected _____ Of The Year. Remember he/she does not
NOUN

know that you think so _____ of him/her. First prize
ADVERB

will be a deluxe, three-speed _____ plus a year's
NOUN

supply of _____. Second prize is a twenty-one-foot
A FOOD

_____. Third prize is a full-color _____.
NOUN   NOUN

plus a set of _____. Each entry must be accompanied by
PLURAL NOUN

a stamped, self-addressed _____. Decision of the
NOUN

_____ will be final and in the event of a tie, duplicate
PLURAL NOUN

_____ wil be awarded.
PLURAL NOUN

MAD LIBS® is fun to play with friends, but you can also play it by yourself!
To begin with, DO NOT look at the story on the page below. Fill in the blanks
on this page with the words called for. Then, using the words you've selected, fill
in the blank spaces in the story.
Now you've created your own hilarious MAD LIB!

MY MUSIC LESSON

NOUN: _____

A FEMALE CELEBRITY: _____

NOUN: _____

PLURAL NOUN: _____

ADJECTIVE: _____

NOUN: _____

PERIOD OF TIME: _____

PLURAL NOUN: _____

LAST NAME OF CELEBRITY: _____

NOUN: _____

PART OF THE BODY: _____

NOUN: _____

NOUN: _____

MY MUSIC LESSON

Every Wednesday when I get home from school I have a piano

lesson. My teacher is a very strict _____.
                                              NOUN

Her name is _____. Our piano is a Steinway
                A FEMALE CELEBRITY

Concert _____ and it has 88 _____.
              NOUN   PLURAL NOUN

It also has a soft pedal and a/an _____ pedal.
                                        ADJECTIVE

When I have a lesson, I sit down on the piano_____
                                                          NOUN

and play for _____. I do scales
                      PERIOD OF TIME

to exercise my _____ and then I usually
                      PLURAL NOUN

play a minuet by Johann Sebastian _____. Teacher
                                    LAST NAME OF CELEBRITY

says I am a natural _____ and have a good musical
                          NOUN

_____. Perhaps when I get better I will become
   PART OF THE BODY

a concert _____ and give a recital in Carnegie
                  NOUN

_____. But I'd rather be a police officer.
      NOUN

From *Goofy Mad Libs*® ● Copyright © 1988 Price Stern Sloan, Inc.,
A member of The Putnam & Grosset Group, New York, New York.

MAD LIBS® is fun to play with friends, but you can also play it by yourself!
To begin with, DO NOT look at the story on the page below. Fill in the blanks
on this page with the words called for. Then, using the words you've selected, fill
in the blank spaces in the story.
Now you've created your own hilarious MAD LIB!

THE FARMER

PLURAL NOUN: _____

NOUN: _____

PLURAL NOUN: _____

ADJECTIVE: _____

PLURAL NOUN: _____

ADJECTIVE: _____

A LIQUID: _____

PLURAL NOUN: _____

NOUN: _____

PLURAL NOUN: _____

ADJECTIVE: _____

THE FARMER

Farmers work very hard planting wheat and _____.
PLURAL NOUN

They begin by plowing their _____ and if they don't
NOUN

have a tractor they use _____. Then they plant
PLURAL NOUN

_____ seeds and by the next Fall they have many acres of
ADJECTIVE

_____. Tomatoes are harder to raise. They grow on
PLURAL NOUN

_____ bushes and the farmer sprays them with
ADJECTIVE

_____ to keep the bugs off. The easiest things to grow
A LIQUID

are green _____ but the farmer must be very careful to
PLURAL NOUN

make sure worms don't get into his_____. Farmers also
NOUN

raise onions, cabbages, lettuce, and _____. But no
PLURAL NOUN

matter what they grow, farmers really lead a/an_____ life.
ADJECTIVE

From *Goofy Mad Libs*® ● Copyright © 1988 Price Stern Sloan, Inc.,

A member of The Putnam & Grosset Group, New York, New York.

MAD LIBS® is fun to play with friends, but you can also play it by yourself! To begin with, DO NOT look at the story on the page below. Fill in the blanks on this page with the words called for. Then, using the words you've selected, fill in the blank spaces in the story.
Now you've created your own hilarious MAD LIB!

HISTORY OF A FAMOUS INVENTION

NOUN: _____

ADJECTIVE: _____

A FAMOUS PERSON: _____

A FAMOUS PERSON: _____

NOUN: _____

PLURAL NOUN: _____

EXCLAMATION: _____

NOUN: _____

ADJECTIVE: _____

PLURAL NOUN: _____

NOUN: _____

PLURAL NOUN: _____

A LIQUID: _____

NOUN: _____

ADJECTIVE: _____

NUMBER: _____

ADVERB: _____

HISTORY OF A FAMOUS INVENTION

The first electric _____ was invented in 1904 by a/an
                              NOUN

_____ young man, named _____. He and
   ADJECTIVE   A FAMOUS PERSON

his brother _____ ran a small _____
                A FAMOUS PERSON   NOUN

repair shop and in their spare time they studied _____.
                                                     PLURAL NOUN

When they started work on their invention, everyone said,

"_____!" You'll never get it off the _____."
      EXCLAMATION   NOUN

But they built a/an _____ model out of old _____
                        ADJECTIVE   PLURAL NOUN

and a used _____. The model worked fine and in ten
                NOUN

minutes it toasted 24 slices of _____. It also used up two
                                   PLURAL NOUN

gallons of _____ an hour, and the top converted into
                A LIQUID

a/an _____. They sold the patent to a/an _____
         NOUN   ADJECTIVE

millionaire for _____ dollars and lived _____
                    NUMBER   ADVERB

ever after.

MAD LIBS® is fun to play with friends, but you can also play it by yourself!
To begin with, DO NOT look at the story on the page below. Fill in the blanks
on this page with the words called for. Then, using the words you've selected, fill
in the blank spaces in the story.
Now you've created your own hilarious MAD LIB!

GEORGE WASHINGTON

NOUN: _____

ADJECTIVE: _____

ADJECTIVE: _____

NOUN: _____

NOUN: _____

EXCLAMATION: _____

VERB (PAST TENSE): _____

NOUN: _____

NOUN: _____

NOUN: _____

NOUN: _____

NOUN: _____

NOUN: _____

GEORGE WASHINGTON

George Washington, the Father of our _____, was a
NOUN

very _____ man. When George was a/an _____
ADJECTIVE ADJECTIVE

boy, he took his _____ and chopped down his father's
NOUN

favorite cherry _____. "_____!" said his
NOUN EXCLAMATION

father, "Who has _____ my _____?"
VERB (PAST TENSE) NOUN

Then he saw George holding a sharp _____ in his hand.
NOUN

"Father," said George. "I cannot tell a lie. I did it with my little

_____." His father smiled and patted little George on
NOUN

the _____. "You are a very honest _____,"
NOUN NOUN

he said, "and some day you may become the first _____
NOUN

of the United States."

MAD LIBS® is fun to play with friends, but you can also play it by yourself!
To begin with, DO NOT look at the story on the page below. Fill in the blanks
on this page with the words called for. Then, using the words you've selected, fill
in the blank spaces in the story.
Now you've created your own hilarious MAD LIB!

THE AMAZING RANDY

PLURAL NOUN: _____

NOUN: _____

NOUN: _____

NOUN: _____

ANIMAL: _____

NOUN: _____

NOUN: _____

ADJECTIVE: _____

NOUN: _____

ADJECTIVE: _____

A LIQUID: _____

A LIQUID: _____

ADJECTIVE: _____

NOUN: _____

A FUNNY WORD: _____

THE AMAZING RANDY

Recently on TV I saw an amazing magician and escape artist. Both of his _____ were laced up in a strait jacket and he was
PLURAL NOUN

suspended by a/an _____ 60 feet in the air over a busy
NOUN

_____. And he escaped! A man who can do that must be
NOUN

a real _____. I saw a magician once who put a/an
NOUN

_____ in a/an _____ and then waved his
ANIMAL   NOUN

magic _____ and made it disappear. I saw another
NOUN

_____ magician who sawed a beautiful _____
ADJECTIVE   NOUN

in half right on the stage. If you practice hard, there are several

_____ magic tricks you can learn to do. For instance,
ADJECTIVE

you can learn how to take a glass of _____ and turn it
A LIQUID

into _____. Or you can wave a/an _____ in
A LIQUID   ADJECTIVE

the air and make it turn into a red _____. All you have to
NOUN

do is memorize the secret magic word, "_____."
A FUNNY WORD

MAD LIBS® is fun to play with friends, but you can also play it by yourself!
To begin with, DO NOT look at the story on the page below. Fill in the blanks
on this page with the words called for. Then, using the words you've selected, fill
in the blank spaces in the story.
Now you've created your own hilarious MAD LIB!

A CHARMING STORY WITH A HAPPY ENDING

NOUN: _____

ADJECTIVE: _____

PLURAL NOUN: _____

ADJECTIVE: _____

PLURAL NOUN: _____

ADJECTIVE: _____

PLURAL NOUN: _____

EXCLAMATION: _____

VERB: _____

VERB: _____

NOUN: _____

NOUN: _____

ADJECTIVE: _____

VERB, PAST TENSE: _____

ADJECTIVE: _____

A CHARMING STORY
WITH A HAPPY ENDING

Once upon a/an _____ there were three little pigs. The
                    NOUN

first little pig was very _____ and he built a house for
                          ADJECTIVE

himself out of _____. The second pig was _____
               PLURAL NOUN   ADJECTIVE

and he built a house out of _____. But the third little pig
                            PLURAL NOUN

was very _____ and he built his house out of genuine
         ADJECTIVE

_____.
   PLURAL NOUN

Well, one day, a mean old wolf came along and saw the houses.

"_____!" he said, "I'll _____ and I'll
  EXCLAMATION   VERB

_____ and I'll blow your house down." And he blew
    VERB

down the first pig's _____ and the second pig's _____.
                         NOUN   NOUN

The two pigs ran to the third pig's house. Thereupon, the wolf began

blowing, but he couldn't blow the third pig's _____
                                                 ADJECTIVE

house. So he _____ off into the forest and the three
             VERB, PAST TENSE

_____ pigs moved to Chicago and went into the sausage
   ADJECTIVE

business.

MAD LIBS® is fun to play with friends, but you can also play it by yourself!
To begin with, DO NOT look at the story on the page below. Fill in the blanks
on this page with the words called for. Then, using the words you've selected, fill
in the blank spaces in the story.
Now you've created your own hilarious MAD LIB!

WEATHER REPORT

PLURAL NOUN: _____

NUMBER: _____

ADJECTIVE: _____

ADJECTIVE: _____

ADVERB: _____

ADJECTIVE: _____

GEOGRAPHICAL LOCATION: _____

ADJECTIVE: _____

GEOGRAPHICAL LOCATION: _____

ADJECTIVE: _____

ADJECTIVE: _____

ADJECTIVE: _____

PLURAL NOUN: _____

PLURAL NOUN: _____

NOUN: _____

WEATHER REPORT

Good evening, ladies and _____. Let's take a look at the
                          PLURAL NOUN

weather picture. Right now the temperature is _____
                                               NUMBER

degrees and there are _____ winds coming from the
                       ADJECTIVE

west. However, according to a report just received, a/an _____
                                                          ADJECTIVE

front is moving down from Canada. This _____ moving
                                        ADVERB

mass of _____ air is headed directly for
              ADJECTIVE

_____ and should result in a/an
  GEOGRAPHICAL LOCATION

_____ pressure area over _____
  ADJECTIVE   GEOGRAPHICAL LOCATION

by early morning. Tomorrow we can expect temperatures in the

_____ forties. Also, it will generally be _____
  ADJECTIVE   ADJECTIVE

and _____ with a chance of scattered _____
      ADJECTIVE   PLURAL NOUN

near the coast. If you are going out, be sure and wear your

_____ and a heavier over-_____, just in case.
  PLURAL NOUN   NOUN

From *Goofy Mad Libs*® ● Copyright © 1988 Price Stern Sloan, Inc.,
A member of The Putnam & Grosset Group, New York, New York.

MAD LIBS® is fun to play with friends, but you can also play it by yourself!
To begin with, DO NOT look at the story on the page below. Fill in the blanks
on this page with the words called for. Then, using the words you've selected, fill
in the blank spaces in the story.
Now you've created your own hilarious MAD LIB!

INDIA

ADJECTIVE: _____

PLURAL NOUN: _____

A PLACE: _____

ADJECTIVE: _____

PLURAL NOUN: _____

PLURAL NOUN: _____

PLURAL NOUN: _____

NOUN: _____

ADVERB: _____

ADJECTIVE: _____

NOUN: _____

PLURAL NOUN: _____

PLURAL NOUN: _____

INDIA

India is a very _____ country located almost directly
        ADJECTIVE

across the world from the United _____ of America.
                                PLURAL NOUN

India is bounded on the north by _____ and on the
                                A PLACE

south by the _____ Ocean.
            ADJECTIVE

Indian women are very beautiful and wear a lot of large

_____ on their arms and often wear long strings of
   PLURAL NOUN

_____ around their necks. They have many religious
   PLURAL NOUN

sects, including Hindus, Brahmins, Mohammedans, and

_____.
   PLURAL NOUN

Many Indians regard the cow as a sacred _____ and
                                        NOUN

cows are allowed to wander _____ about the streets.
                          ADVERB

One Indian caste is called the Untouchables. The _____
                                                ADJECTIVE

Untouchables sit in the city _____ and beg tourists to
                            NOUN

give them _____. Unlike American Indians, India
         PLURAL NOUN

Indians never wear _____.
                  PLURAL NOUN

MAD LIBS® is fun to play with friends, but you can also play it by yourself!
To begin with, DO NOT look at the story on the page below. Fill in the blanks
on this page with the words called for. Then, using the words you've selected, fill
in the blank spaces in the story.
Now you've created your own hilarious MAD LIB!

IRELAND

A PLACE: _____

PLURAL NOUN: _____

ADJECTIVE: _____

PLURAL NOUN: _____

NOUN: _____

PLURAL NOUN: _____

PLURAL NOUN: _____

NOUN: _____

NOUN: _____

A PLACE: _____

PLURAL NOUN: _____

PLURAL NOUN: _____

IRELAND

Ireland is a beautiful, green island lying directly west of _____.
A PLACE

In 250 B.C., Ireland was inhabited by short, dark _____
PLURAL NOUN

who were later called "Picts." They intermarried with _____
ADJECTIVE

Vikings and with Celts who were _____ from Northern
PLURAL NOUN

Europe. In 1846, a blight ruined the _____ crop in
NOUN

Ireland and over a million Irishmen migrated to the United States.

Many of their descendants have become very important American

_____.
PLURAL NOUN

The Irish are noted for their poetry and songs. Some of these Irish

songs are: "When Irish _____ are Smiling," "Did Your
PLURAL NOUN

_____ Come from Ireland?" and "McNamara's
NOUN

_____."
NOUN

Thousands of American tourists go to Ireland every year to visit its

capital, _____, and buy Irish linen _____,
A PLACE   PLURAL NOUN

and see the beautiful _____ and lakes.
PLURAL NOUN

MAD LIBS ® is fun to play with friends, but you can also play it by yourself!
To begin with, DO NOT look at the story on the page below. Fill in the blanks
on this page with the words called for. Then, using the words you've selected, fill
in the blank spaces in the story.
Now you've created your own hilarious MAD LIB!

TARZAN

ADJECTIVE: _____

PLURAL NOUN: _____

NOUN: _____

ADJECTIVE: _____

A PLACE: _____

PLURAL NOUN: _____

NOUN: _____

A FUNNY NOISE: _____

ADJECTIVE: _____

NOUN: _____

ADJECTIVE: _____

PLURAL NOUN: _____

A PERSON: _____

TARZAN

One of the most _____ characters in fiction is called
                    ADJECTIVE

"Tarzan of the _____." Tarzan was raised by a/an
               PLURAL NOUN

_____ and lives in a/an _____ jungle in the
      NOUN   ADJECTIVE

heart of darkest _____. He spends most of his time
                    A PLACE

eating_____ and swinging from tree to_____.
         PLURAL NOUN   NOUN

Whenever he gets angry, he beats on his chest and says,

"_____!" This is his war cry. Tarzan always dresses in
   A FUNNY NOISE

_____ shorts made from the skin of a/an _____,
   ADJECTIVE   NOUN

and his best friend is a/an _____ chimpanzee named
                               ADJECTIVE

Cheetah. He is supposed to be able to speak to elephants and

_____. In the movies, Tarzan is played by _____.
   PLURAL NOUN   A PERSON

MAD LIBS® is fun to play with friends, but you can also play it by yourself!
To begin with, DO NOT look at the story on the page below. Fill in the blanks
on this page with the words called for. Then, using the words you've selected, fill
in the blank spaces in the story.
Now you've created your own hilarious MAD LIB!

DOGS

NOUN: _____

ADJECTIVE: _____

ADJECTIVE: _____

NOUN: _____

NOUN: _____

ADVERB: _____

NOUN: _____

NOUN: _____

A COLOR: _____

ADJECTIVE: _____

ADJECTIVE: _____

A NUMBER: _____

ADJECTIVE: _____

PLURAL NOUN: _____

ADJECTIVE: _____

NOUN: _____

DOGS

It's often been said that "A Dog is Man's Best _____."
                                                    NOUN

Dogs are very _____ and can be taught many
                    ADJECTIVE

_____ tricks. A dog can be trained to carry a/an
   ADJECTIVE

_____ in his mouth. And if you throw a/an _____,
        NOUN   NOUN

he will run and fetch it. Dogs will also bark _____ if a
                                                      ADVERB

burglar tries to break into your _____ during the night.
                                          NOUN

One of the most popular canine pets is the _____
                                                    NOUN

Spaniel. Spaniels have curly _____ coats and
                                    A COLOR

_____ ears. They also have very _____
   ADJECTIVE   ADJECTIVE

dispositions and live to be _____ years old. Other
                                  A NUMBER

popular dogs are the _____ Terriers, German
                            ADJECTIVE

_____, and the _____ Poodle. Every home
   PLURAL NOUN   ADJECTIVE

should have a loyal dog for a/an _____.
                                        NOUN

MAD LIBS® is fun to play with friends, but you can also play it by yourself! To begin with, DO NOT look at the story on the page below. Fill in the blanks on this page with the words called for. Then, using the words you've selected, fill in the blank spaces in the story.
Now you've created your own hilarious MAD LIB!

WHAT DO YOU DO WHEN YOU HAVE A COLD?

NOUN:_____

NOUN:_____

PLURAL NOUN:_____

NOUN:_____

A LIQUID:_____

NOUN:_____

NOUN:_____

NOUN:_____

A NUMBER:_____

NOUN:_____

EXCLAMATION:_____

NOUN:_____

ADJECTIVE:_____

ADJECTIVE:_____

WHAT DO YOU DO WHEN YOU HAVE A COLD?

You can always tell when you're getting a cold because your

_____ will feel stuffy and you will have a/an
NOUN

_____ ache. The first thing to do is take a couple of
NOUN

_____. Then get into your _____ and
PLURAL NOUN   NOUN

rest, and drink plenty of _____. Sometimes it's fun
A LIQUID

being sick. Food is brought to you on a/an _____ so you
NOUN

can eat and watch TV, and your temperature is taken by putting a/an

_____ in your _____. If your tempera-
NOUN   NOUN

ture goes over _____ degrees, a doctor should be called.
A NUMBER

He will thump you on the _____ and say,
NOUN

"_____!" Then he will ask you what
EXCLAMATION

_____ you ate the night before and x-ray your stomach.
NOUN

Finally, he will give you _____ advice on how to get
ADJECTIVE

well. If you do just what he says, you'll feel _____ in no
ADJECTIVE

time at all.

From *Goofy Mad Libs*® ● Copyright © 1988 Price Stern Sloan, Inc.,

A member of The Putnam & Grosset Group, New York, New York.

MAD LIBS® is fun to play with friends, but you can also play it by yourself! To begin with, DO NOT look at the story on the page below. Fill in the blanks on this page with the words called for. Then, using the words you've selected, fill in the blank spaces in the story.
Now you've created your own hilarious MAD LIB!

SPECIAL SPRING CLOTHING SALE

MALE NAME:_____

ADJECTIVE:_____

A CITY:_____

ADJECTIVE:_____

ADJECTIVE:_____

PLURAL NOUN:_____

PLURAL NOUN:_____

PLURAL NOUN:_____

PLURAL NOUN:_____

A COLOR:_____

ADJECTIVE:_____

ADJECTIVE:_____

PLURAL NOUN:_____

ADJECTIVE:_____

SPECIAL SPRING SALE OF CLOTHING

_____ has announced that his _____
         MALE NAME   ADJECTIVE

clothing store in the heart of downtown _____ is having
                                                          A CITY

a/an _____ sale of all merchandise, including
              ADJECTIVE

_____ suits and slightly irregular
         ADJECTIVE

_____. Men's cable-knit _____, only
   PLURAL NOUN   PLURAL NOUN

$15.99. Hand-woven Italian _____, half-price. Double-
                                          PLURAL NOUN

breasted cashmere _____, $50.00. Genuine imported
                              PLURAL NOUN

_____ _____ shoes,
         A COLOR   ADJECTIVE

_____ handkerchiefs, and women's embroidered
    ADJECTIVE

_____, all at rock-bottom prices. This is a chance to get
   PLURAL NOUN

some really _____ bargains.
                   ADJECTIVE

MAD LIBS® is fun to play with friends, but you can also play it by yourself!
To begin with, DO NOT look at the story on the page below. Fill in the blanks
on this page with the words called for. Then, using the words you've selected, fill
in the blank spaces in the story.
Now you've created your own hilarious MAD LIB!

COMMERCIAL FOR FACE CREAM

PLURAL NOUN: _____

NOUN: _____

NUMBER: _____

ADJECTIVE: _____

NOUN: _____

NOUN: _____

ADJECTIVE: _____

FILM STAR: _____

ADJECTIVE: _____

PLURAL NOUN: _____

ADJECTIVE: _____

NOUN: _____

NUMBER: _____

NOUN: _____

COMMERCIAL FOR FACE CREAM

And now, ladies and _____, an important commercial

PLURAL NOUN

message from our _____, the manufacturer of new,

NOUN

improved ALL-GOO, the face cream for women over_____.

NUMBER

ALL-GOO now contains a new _____ ingredient called

ADJECTIVE

"Hexa-mone," which is made from distilled _____

NOUN

juice. If you rub ALL-GOO on your _____ every

NOUN

evening, your complexion will look as _____ as a daisy.

ADJECTIVE

The famous Hollywood star, _____, says, "I use ALL-

FILM STAR

GOO every day, and my complexion is always _____

ADJECTIVE

and my _____ always have a youthful glow." Yes, ALL-

PLURAL NOUN

GOO is the _____ cream of the stars. Remember, if you

ADJECTIVE

want a softer, smoother _____, get ALL-GOO in the

NOUN

handy_____-pound size at your friendly neighborhood

NUMBER

_____ store.

NOUN

From *Goofy Mad Libs*® ● Copyright © 1988 Price Stern Sloan, Inc.,

A member of The Putnam & Grosset Group, New York, New York.

MAD LIBS®

World's Greatest Word Game

A super silly way to fill in the _____!

(plural noun)

by Roger Price & Leonard Stern

MAD LIBS® is fun to play with friends, but you can also play it by yourself!

To begin with, DO NOT look at the story on the page below. Fill in the blanks on this page with the words called for. Then, using the words you've selected, fill in the blank spaces in the story. Now you've created your own hilarious MAD LIB!

PAUL REVERE

A STATE: _____

ADJECTIVE: _____

NOUN: _____

A NATIONALITY: _____

NOUN: _____

A LIQUID: _____

A PLACE: _____

NOUN: _____

NOUN: _____

NOUN: _____

ADVERB: _____

PLURAL NOUN: _____

SAME PLURAL NOUN: _____

A CELEBRITY: _____

PAUL REVERE

Paul Revere was born in Boston, _____ in 1735. His
                                       A STATE

father taught him to work with metals, and he soon became a/an

_____ _____. He was a soldier in the
   ADJECTIVE   NOUN

French and _____ War and was at the famous Boston
            A NATIONALITY

_____ Party when Americans dressed as Indians
      NOUN

dumped tons of _____ into the ocean. On April 18,
                  A LIQUID

1775, Paul Revere waited in _____ for a signal light
                              A PLACE

from a church tower. The signal was to be one if by _____,
                                                        NOUN

two if by _____.
            NOUN

When he got the message, he mounted his faithful _____
                                                      NOUN

and rode off _____. On the way he kept yelling, "The
                ADVERB

_____ are coming! The _____ are
 PLURAL NOUN   SAME PLURAL NOUN

coming!"

This was the beginning of the American War for Independence from

King _____.
       A CELEBRITY

From *Off-The-Wall Mad Libs*® ● Copyright © 1988, 1982, 1970 Price Stern Sloan, Inc.,
A member of The Putnam & Grosset Group, New York, New York.

MAD LIBS® is fun to play with friends, but you can also play it by yourself!
To begin with, DO NOT look at the story on the page below. Fill in the blanks
on this page with the words called for. Then, using the words you've selected, fill
in the blank spaces in the story.
Now you've created your own hilarious MAD LIB!

ELIZABETH THE FIRST

NOUN: _____

ADJECTIVE (SUPERLATIVE): _____

NOUN: _____

ADJECTIVE: _____

ADJECTIVE: _____

ADVERB: _____

ADJECTIVE: _____

NAME OF CELEBRITY: _____

CELEBRITY: _____

A PERSON: _____

ADJECTIVE: _____

ELIZABETH THE FIRST

Elizabeth, the Tudor _____ of England, was probably
NOUN

the _____ ruler the British ever had. Elizabeth was
ADJECTIVE (SUPERLATIVE)

the daughter of Henry the Eighth and Anne Boleyn. Later Anne had

her _____ chopped off by Henry.
NOUN

Elizabeth was born in 1533 and became queen when she was 25. She

was a/an _____ Protestant and persecuted the _____
ADJECTIVE   ADJECTIVE

Catholics _____. In 1588 the _____ armada
ADVERB   ADJECTIVE

attacked England. But the English fleet, commanded by

_____ and _____, defeated
NAME OF CELEBRITY   CELEBRITY

them. Elizabeth ruled for 45 years, and during her reign England

prospered and produced Shakespeare, Francis Bacon, and

_____. Elizabeth never married, which is why she
A PERSON

is sometimes called the _____ Queen.
ADJECTIVE

MAD LIBS® is fun to play with friends, but you can also play it by yourself!
To begin with, DO NOT look at the story on the page below. Fill in the blanks
on this page with the words called for. Then, using the words you've selected, fill
in the blank spaces in the story.
Now you've created your own hilarious MAD LIB!

REPORT BY STUDENT PROTEST COMMITTEE

FULL NAME OF SCHOOL: _____

ADJECTIVE: _____

PLURAL NOUN: _____

NAME OF PERSON IN ROOM: _____

PART OF THE BODY: _____

ARTICLE OF CLOTHING: _____

PLURAL NOUN: _____

NOUN: _____

NOUN: _____

ADJECTIVE: _____

ADJECTIVE: _____

PLURAL NOUN: _____

1

REPORT BY STUDENT PROTEST COMMITTEE

Fellow Students of_____! We members of the
                    FULL NAME OF SCHOOL

Students for a/an _____ Society are meeting here to decide
                    ADJECTIVE

what action to take about the Dean of_____. He has just
                                        PLURAL NOUN

fired our friend, Professor _____, because he
                            NAME OF PERSON IN ROOM

wore his_____ long, and because he dressed in
            PART OF THE BODY

_____ and wore old _____. Next
    ARTICLE OF CLOTHING   PLURAL NOUN

week we are going to protest by taking over the _____
                                                    NOUN

building and kidnapping the Assistant _____. We also
                                            NOUN

will demand that all students have the right to wear_____
                                                        ADJECTIVE

hair and _____ beards. Remember our slogan: "Down
            ADJECTIVE

with _____."
        PLURAL NOUN

MAD LIBS® is fun to play with friends, but you can also play it by yourself!
To begin with, DO NOT look at the story on the page below. Fill in the blanks
on this page with the words called for. Then, using the words you've selected, fill
in the blank spaces in the story.
Now you've created your own hilarious MAD LIB!

ALEXANDER THE GREAT

NOUN: _____

NOUN: _____

NAME OF GREEK PERSON: _____

NOUN: _____

A FAMOUS PERSON: _____

A PLACE: _____

NOUN: _____

A SILLY WORD: _____

PLURAL NOUN: _____

A LIQUID: _____

PART OF THE BODY: _____

PLURAL NOUN: _____

ALEXANDER THE GREAT

In 356 B.C., Phillip of Macedonia, the ruler of a province in northern Greece, became the father of a bouncing baby _____
NOUN
named Alexander. Alexander's teacher was Aristotle, the famous _____. When he was 20 years old, his father was
NOUN
murdered by _____, after which he became
NAME OF GREEK PERSON
_____ of all Macedonia. In 334 he invaded Persia and
NOUN
defeated _____ at the battle of _____.
A FAMOUS PERSON   A PLACE
Later, at Arbela, he won his most important victory over Darius, the Third. This made him _____ _____
NOUN   A SILLY WORD
over all Persians. Then he marched to India, and many of his _____ died. After that Alexander began drinking too
PLURAL NOUN
much _____ and at the age of 33 he died of an infection
A LIQUID
in the _____. His last words are reported to have
PART OF THE BODY
been, "There are no more _____ to conquer."
PLURAL NOUN

MAD LIBS® is fun to play with friends, but you can also play it by yourself!
To begin with, DO NOT look at the story on the page below. Fill in the blanks
on this page with the words called for. Then, using the words you've selected, fill
in the blank spaces in the story.
Now you've created your own hilarious MAD LIB!

EASTER

PLURAL NOUN: _____

NUMBER: _____

ADJECTIVE: _____

NOUN: _____

A GAME: _____

ADJECTIVE: _____

PLURAL NOUN: _____

ADJECTIVE: _____

ADJECTIVE: _____

A LIQUID: _____

NOUN: _____

A LIQUID: _____

ADJECTIVE: _____

EASTER

Easter vacations usually fall around Easter time.

The schools are closed and all the _____ get
                                    PLURAL NOUN

_____ weeks off. The _____ teachers also
     NUMBER   ADJECTIVE

get a vacation. There are a lot of things to do on Easter vacation.

Some kids loaf around and watch the _____. Others get
                                         NOUN

outside and play _____, while more ambitious students
                     A GAME

spend their time studying their_____ books so they will
                                  ADJECTIVE

grow up to become _____. Little kids also color
                       PLURAL NOUN

_____ eggs.
   ADJECTIVE

Here's how you color an egg: First mix a package of_____
                                                        ADJECTIVE

dye in a bowl full of _____. Then dip the _____
                          A LIQUID   NOUN

in the bowl and rinse it off with _____. Then after it
                                      A LIQUID

dries, you can paint on it with a brush. Then you show it to your

friends who will say, "Boy, what a/an _____ egg!"
                                          ADJECTIVE

MAD LIBS® is fun to play with friends, but you can also play it by yourself!
To begin with, DO NOT look at the story on the page below. Fill in the blanks
on this page with the words called for. Then, using the words you've selected, fill
in the blank spaces in the story.
Now you've created your own hilarious MAD LIB!

ALBERT EINSTEIN

MALE CELEBRITY: _____

FEMALE CELEBRITY: _____

NOUN: _____

PLURAL NOUN: _____

ADJECTIVE: _____

PLURAL NOUN: _____

ADJECTIVE: _____

PLURAL NOUN: _____

NOUN: _____

A PLACE: _____

PLURAL NOUN: _____

NOUN: _____

JOB CLASSIFICATION (PLURAL): _____

ALBERT EINSTEIN

Albert Einstein was born in Ulm, Germany in 1879, the son of

_____ and _____. In 1902
　　　MALE CELEBRITY　　　　　　　　FEMALE CELEBRITY

he had a job as assistant _____ in the Swiss patent office
　　　　　　　　　　　　　　NOUN

and attended the University of Zurich. There he began studying

atoms, molecules, and _____. He evolved his famous
　　　　　　　　　　　PLURAL NOUN

theory of _____ relativity, which explained the phe-
　　　　　ADJECTIVE

nomena of subatomic _____ and _____
　　　　　　　　　　PLURAL NOUN　　　　　　　　ADJECTIVE

magnetism. In 1921 he won the Nobel Prize for _____
　　　　　　　　　　　　　　　　　　　　　　PLURAL NOUN

and was director of theoretical physics at the Kaiser Wilhelm

_____ in Berlin. In 1933, when Hitler became Chan-
　　　NOUN

cellor of _____, he came to America to take a post at the
　　　　　A PLACE

Princeton Institute for _____ where his theories helped
　　　　　　　　　　　PLURAL NOUN

America devise the first atomic _____. There is no
　　　　　　　　　　　　　　　NOUN

question about it, Einstein was one of the most brilliant

_____ of our time.
　JOB CLASSIFICATION (PLURAL)

From *Off-The-Wall Mad Libs*® ● Copyright © 1988, 1982, 1970 Price Stern Sloan, Inc.,

A member of The Putnam & Grosset Group, New York, New York.

MAD LIBS® is fun to play with friends, but you can also play it by yourself!
To begin with, DO NOT look at the story on the page below. Fill in the blanks
on this page with the words called for. Then, using the words you've selected, fill
in the blank spaces in the story.
Now you've created your own hilarious MAD LIB!

ROCK MUSIC

SOMEONE'S LAST NAME: _____

ANOTHER LAST NAME: _____

ADJECTIVE: _____

PLURAL NOUN: _____

PLURAL NOUN: _____

PLURAL NAME OF ANIMAL: _____

NAME OF CELEBRITY: _____

PLURAL NOUN: _____

PLURAL NOUN: _____

NOUN: _____

NOUN: _____

PLURAL NOUN: _____

ROCK MUSIC

Young people today would rather listen to a good rock music concert than to Johann Sebastian _____ or to

SOMEONE'S LAST NAME

Ludvig von _____.

ANOTHER LAST NAME

Rock music is played by _____ groups of young men

ADJECTIVE

who wear their hair below their _____. They also wear

PLURAL NOUN

very odd and colorful _____ and often have beards.

PLURAL NOUN

The groups have attractive names such as "The_____"

PLURAL NAME OF ANIMAL

or "_____ and The Three _____."

NAME OF CELEBRITY   PLURAL NOUN

They usually play electric _____. One member of the

PLURAL NOUN

group usually sits on a raised platform and sets the rhythm by

beating his _____. The songs they sing are mostly about

NOUN

some fellow who has been rejected by his _____. They

NOUN

are very sad, and when young girls hear them they often get tears in

their _____.

PLURAL NOUN

MAD LIBS® is fun to play with friends, but you can also play it by yourself!
To begin with, DO NOT look at the story on the page below. Fill in the blanks
on this page with the words called for. Then, using the words you've selected, fill
in the blank spaces in the story.
Now you've created your own hilarious MAD LIB!

BENJAMIN FRANKLIN

VERB (PRESENT TENSE): _____

PLURAL NOUN: _____

NOUN: _____

NOUN: _____

ADJECTIVE: _____

ADVERB: _____

ADJECTIVE: _____

NOUN: _____

NOUN: _____

PLURAL NOUN: _____

ADJECTIVE: _____

AN ABSTRACT NOUN
(AS OPPOSED TO A CONCRETE NOUN): _____

BENJAMIN FRANKLIN

Benjamin Franklin left school at the age of 10 to _____
VERB (PRESENT TENSE)

for his father who made candles, soap, and _____ in a
PLURAL NOUN

little shop in Boston. In 1723, when Franklin was 17, he went to

Philadelphia carrying a loaf of _____ under his arm. He
NOUN

got a job as an apprentice _____ and soon became the
NOUN

editor of the Pennsylvania Gazette, a/an _____ publi-
ADJECTIVE

cation. He worked _____ and in 1732 he published the
ADVERB

_____ book called "Poor Richard's _____."
ADJECTIVE   NOUN

He then became interested in science, and during a thunderstorm he

flew a/an _____ attached to a string and proved that
NOUN

lightning and electricity were the same thing. He also invented the

harmonica, bifocal _____, and started our postal sys-
PLURAL NOUN

tem. In 1776 he became the American Ambassador to France and

did much to help the _____ cause of American liberty.
ADJECTIVE

Franklin was one of the most famous signers of the Declaration of

_____.
AN ABSTRACT NOUN (AS OPPOSED TO A CONCRETE NOUN)

MAD LIBS® is fun to play with friends, but you can also play it by yourself!
To begin with, DO NOT look at the story on the page below. Fill in the blanks
on this page with the words called for. Then, using the words you've selected, fill
in the blank spaces in the story.
Now you've created your own hilarious MAD LIB!

NAPOLEON

NOUN: _____

NOUN: _____

ADJECTIVE: _____

ADJECTIVE: _____

ADJECTIVE: _____

NOUN: _____

ITALIAN WORD: _____

PLURAL NOUN: _____

ADJECTIVE: _____

PLURAL NOUN: _____

PLURAL NOUN: _____

PLURAL NOUN: _____

VERB (PAST TENSE): _____

NOUN: _____

ADJECTIVE: _____

A CITY: _____

NAPOLEON

Although he was Emperor of France, Napoleon Bonaparte was

actually a Corsican, born on a small _____ in the
                                         NOUN

Mediterranean Sea. When he was 10 years old, Napoleon was sent

to a military _____ school in France, where his
                     NOUN

_____ stature earned him the nickname of "The
     ADJECTIVE

_____ Corporal."
     ADJECTIVE

At 24 he was made a/an _____ General and married
                              ADJECTIVE

Josephine, the daughter of a well-known Parisian _____.
                                                        NOUN

Soon after that he defeated the Italians at _____ and in
                                                 ITALIAN WORD

1804 was proclaimed Emperor of all the _____. But he
                                            PLURAL NOUN

made a/an _____ and attacked Russia. He reached Moscow,
               ADJECTIVE

but the _____ had burned all their _____
             PLURAL NOUN   PLURAL NOUN

and his men got frozen _____. In 1914 he was
                              PLURAL NOUN

_____ and sent to Elba. But a year later he came
  VERB (PAST TENSE)

back to France and for 100 days was again the _____.
                                                     NOUN

However, he was defeated at Waterloo and imprisoned on the island

of St. Helena, a/an _____ place which resembled
                          ADJECTIVE

_____.
  A CITY

MAD LIBS® is fun to play with friends, but you can also play it by yourself! To begin with, DO NOT look at the story on the page below. Fill in the blanks on this page with the words called for. Then, using the words you've selected, fill in the blank spaces in the story.
Now you've created your own hilarious MAD LIB!

OUR SCHOOL

NAME OF SCHOOL: _____

ADJECTIVE (SUPERLATIVE): _____

ADJECTIVE: _____

NUMBER: _____

NUMBER: _____

PLURAL NOUN: _____

SAME PLURAL NOUN: _____

ADJECTIVE: _____

PLURAL NOUN: _____

NOUN: _____

A LIQUID: _____

A FAMOUS PERSON: _____

NOUN: _____

NOUN: _____

ADJECTIVE: _____

OUR SCHOOL

_____ is one of America's _____
NAME OF SCHOOL   ADJECTIVE (SUPERLATIVE)

institutions of _____ learning.
                    ADJECTIVE

The student body is composed of _____ males and
                                      NUMBER

_____ _____. The _____
      NUMBER   PLURAL NOUN   SAME PLURAL NOUN

make the best grades. Students can eat lunch in the _____
                                                         ADJECTIVE

school cafeteria which features boiled _____ and
                                            PLURAL NOUN

_____ sandwiches, with all the _____ they
      NOUN   A LIQUID

can drink, for only 74 cents. The principal of the school,

_____, is raising money to build a new
    A FAMOUS PERSON

_____ laboratory and a new football _____.
      NOUN   NOUN

Any student who goes to this school can consider himself very

_____.
    ADJECTIVE

MAD LIBS® is fun to play with friends, but you can also play it by yourself!
To begin with, DO NOT look at the story on the page below. Fill in the blanks
on this page with the words called for. Then, using the words you've selected, fill
in the blank spaces in the story.
Now you've created your own hilarious MAD LIB!

CHARLEMAGNE

ADJECTIVE: _____

NATIONALITY (PLURAL): _____

NOUN: _____

ADJECTIVE: _____

NOUN: _____

NOUN: _____

PLURAL NOUN: _____

PLURAL NOUN: _____

A TOWN: _____

ADJECTIVE: _____

PLURAL NOUN: _____

ADJECTIVE: _____

CHARLEMAGNE

Charlemagne was the _____ King of the Franks
ADJECTIVE

and _____. In 800 A.D. he was crowned
NATIONALITY (PLURAL)

Emperor of the Holy Roman _____ by Pope Leo the
NOUN

Third. He was born in 742. His father was Pepin the_____,
ADJECTIVE

and his grandfather was Charles the _____. Charle-
NOUN

magne converted thousands of Saxons, who were_____
NOUN

worshippers, to Christianity. He converted them by cutting off their

_____ and setting fire to their _____.
PLURAL NOUN   PLURAL NOUN

In 778 he invaded Spain but was defeated by the Moors at

_____. Charlemagne was uneducated but he had great
A TOWN

respect for education and established many _____
ADJECTIVE

schools. And he was known for the justice of his _____
PLURAL NOUN

and his kindness to _____ people.
ADJECTIVE

From *Off-The-Wall Mad Libs*® ● Copyright © 1988, 1982, 1970 Price Stern Sloan, Inc.,

A member of The Putnam & Grosset Group, New York, New York.

MAD LIBS® is fun to play with friends, but you can also play it by yourself! To begin with, DO NOT look at the story on the page below. Fill in the blanks on this page with the words called for. Then, using the words you've selected, fill in the blank spaces in the story.

Now you've created your own hilarious MAD LIB!

GEORGE WASHINGTON CARVER

ADJECTIVE: _____

NOUN: _____

PLURAL NOUN: _____

ADJECTIVE: _____

PLURAL NOUN: _____

SOMETHING TO EAT: _____

A PLACE: _____

A COLOR: _____

PLURAL NOUN: _____

GEORGE WASHINGTON CARVER

George Washington Carver was a very _____ black
                                      ADJECTIVE

scientist. He was born a/an _____ in Missouri and grad-
                               NOUN

uated from Iowa State College with high _____. He then
                                          PLURAL NOUN

worked at the Tuskegee Institute as head of the _____
                                                   ADJECTIVE

Department and did much research in the field of _____.
                                                    PLURAL NOUN

He discovered many new uses for the peanut, the soy bean, and the

_____. He also improved the production of cotton
  SOMETHING TO EAT

and helped the entire economy of _____. George
                                    A PLACE

Washington Carver was looked up to as an inspiration by all

_____ people. His death in 1943 was a loss to science
  A COLOR

and to _____ everywhere.
         PLURAL NOUN

MAD LIBS® is fun to play with friends, but you can also play it by yourself!
To begin with, DO NOT look at the story on the page below. Fill in the blanks
on this page with the words called for. Then, using the words you've selected, fill
in the blank spaces in the story.
Now you've created your own hilarious MAD LIB!

HOW TO BE A PHOTOGRAPHER

ADJECTIVE: _____

PLURAL NOUN: _____

PLURAL NOUN: _____

ADJECTIVE: _____

NOUN: _____

NOUN: _____

ADJECTIVE: _____

NOUN: _____

PLURAL NOUN: _____

PLURAL NOUN: _____

ADVERB: _____

NUMBER: _____

HOW TO BE A PHOTOGRAPHER

Many _____ photographers make big money photo-
ADJECTIVE

graphing _____ and beautiful _____. They
PLURAL NOUN   PLURAL NOUN

sell the prints to _____ magazines or to agencies who
ADJECTIVE

use them in _____ advertisements. To be a photo-
NOUN

grapher, you have to have a/an _____ camera. You also
NOUN

need a/an _____ meter and filters and a special close-up
ADJECTIVE

_____. Then you either hire professional _____
NOUN   PLURAL NOUN

or go out and snap candid pictures of ordinary _____.
PLURAL NOUN

But if you want to have a career, you must study very _____
ADVERB

for at least _____ years.
NUMBER

MAD LIBS® is fun to play with friends, but you can also play it by yourself!
To begin with, DO NOT look at the story on the page below. Fill in the blanks
on this page with the words called for. Then, using the words you've selected, fill
in the blank spaces in the story.
Now you've created your own hilarious MAD LIB!

JULIUS CAESAR

A LETTER: _____

ADJECTIVE: _____

PLURAL NOUN: _____

ADVERB: _____

A GEOGRAPHICAL LOCATION: _____

A TITLE: _____

NOUN: _____

NOUN: _____

AN ITALIAN WORD: _____

NOUN: _____

NOUN: _____

NAME OF WELL-KNOWN ITALIAN: _____

JULIUS CAESAR

Julius Caesar was born in 102 B._____. He was a/an
                                    A LETTER

_____ General and between 49 and 58 B.C. he defeated
    ADJECTIVE

the Gauls, the Goths, and the _____. After that, he
                                PLURAL NOUN

_____ became more famous and defeated Pompey at
     ADVERB

the battle of _____ at Pharsala. The Romans
              A GEOGRAPHICAL LOCATION

then elected him permanent _____; and he used to walk
                              A TITLE

around wearing a circle of ivy leaves on his _____. Then
                                                NOUN

Caesar went to Egypt where he met Cleopatra, the teenage Egyptian

_____. When he conquered the Syrians in 46 B.C., he
    NOUN

sent back a message saying, "Veni, Vedi _____." In 44
                                         AN ITALIAN WORD

B.C. a soothsayer told Caesar to "Beware the Ides of _____,"
                                                        NOUN

but he ignored the warning and in March he was stabbed in the

_____ by a group of senators. His last words were, "Et
    NOUN

tu _____?"
   NAME OF WELL-KNOWN ITALIAN

MAD LIBS® is fun to play with friends, but you can also play it by yourself! To begin with, DO NOT look at the story on the page below. Fill in the blanks on this page with the words called for. Then, using the words you've selected, fill in the blank spaces in the story.
Now you've created your own hilarious MAD LIB!

LITTLE RED RIDING HOOD

A COLOR: _____

PLURAL NOUN: _____

ADJECTIVE: _____

EXCLAMATION: _____

PET NAME: _____

VERB (PAST TENSE): _____

PLURAL NOUN: _____

VERB (PRESENT TENSE): _____

PLURAL NOUN: _____

VERB (PRESENT TENSE): _____

PLURAL NOUN: _____

LITTLE RED RIDING HOOD

One day Little _____ Riding Hood was going through
                 A COLOR

the forest carrying a basket of _____ for her grand-
                            PLURAL NOUN

mother. Suddenly she met a big _____ wolf.
                            ADJECTIVE

"_____!" said the wolf. "Where are you going,
   EXCLAMATION

little _____?"
     PET NAME

"I'm going to my grandmother's house," said she. Then the wolf

_____ away. When Miss Riding Hood got to
    VERB (PAST TENSE)

her grandmother's house, the wolf was in bed dressed like her

grandmother. "My, grandmother," she said, "What big_____
                                    PLURAL NOUN

you have." "The better to_____ you with," said the
                 VERB (PRESTENT TENSE)

wolf. "And grandmother," she said, "What big _____
                              PLURAL NOUN

you have." The wolf said, "The better to_____ you
                     VERB (PRESENT TENSE)

with." And then she said, "What big _____ you have,
                       PLURAL NOUN

Grandmother." But the wolf said nothing. He had just died of

indigestion from eating grandmother.

MAD LIBS® is fun to play with friends, but you can also play it by yourself! To begin with, DO NOT look at the story on the page below. Fill in the blanks on this page with the words called for. Then, using the words you've selected, fill in the blank spaces in the story.
Now you've created your own hilarious MAD LIB!

INTRODUCTION TO A KIDDY SHOW

ADJECTIVE:_____

NAME OF PERSON IN ROOM:_____

NUMBER:_____

PLURAL NOUN:_____

AN ANIMAL:_____

A BIRD:_____

NONSENSE WORD:_____

NOUN:_____

A LANGUAGE:_____

NOUN:_____

NUMBER:_____

ADJECTIVE:_____

INTRODUCTION TO A KIDDY SHOW

Hi there all you _____ little boys and girls! This is your
ADJECTIVE

old TV buddy, _____, with another
NAME OF PERSON IN ROOM

_____-hour program of fun and films and
NUMBER

_____ for all of you. And we have a lot of great cartoons
PLURAL NOUN

and videos. We will start with a cartoon about Mickey

_____ and Donald _____. Then we'll
AN ANIMAL   A BIRD

have a commercial for a new toy called _____. It will
NONSENSE WORD

teach you how to build a _____ and how to speak
NOUN

_____ before you even start school. Next we'll have a
A LANGUAGE

cartoon about Bullwinkle and Rocky, the Flying

_____. And after that, _____ more
NOUN   NUMBER

_____ commercials. Wow!
ADJECTIVE

MAD LIBS® is fun to play with friends, but you can also play it by yourself!
To begin with, DO NOT look at the story on the page below. Fill in the blanks
on this page with the words called for. Then, using the words you've selected, fill
in the blank spaces in the story.
Now you've created your own hilarious MAD LIB!

THE THREE LITTLE PIGS

ADJECTIVE: _____

PLURAL NOUN: _____

ADVERB: _____

PLURAL NOUN: _____

ADJECTIVE: _____

PLURAL NOUN: _____

A LIQUID: _____

VERB (PAST TENSE): _____

VERB (PAST TENSE): _____

NOUN: _____

VERB (PAST TENSE): _____

NOUN: _____

PLURAL NOUN: _____

THE THREE LITTLE PIGS

Once upon a time there were three little pigs who decided to build

themselves houses. The first pig was _____ and he built
ADJECTIVE

his house out of _____. The second pig worked very
PLURAL NOUN

_____ and built a house out of _____. But
ADVERB   PLURAL NOUN

the third pig was _____. He built his house out of
ADJECTIVE

_____ and _____.
PLURAL NOUN   A LIQUID

Then one day a big wolf came along. When he saw the first pig's

house he _____ and he _____
VERB (PAST TENSE)   VERB (PAST TENSE)

until he blew it down. Then he blew down the second pig's

_____. But no matter how hard he _____,
NOUN   VERB (PAST TENSE)

he couldn't blow down the third pig's _____.
NOUN

MORAL: Once the _____ come home to roost, it's too
PLURAL NOUN

late to whitewash the walls.

MAD LIBS® is fun to play with friends, but you can also play it by yourself!
To begin with, DO NOT look at the story on the page below. Fill in the blanks
on this page with the words called for. Then, using the words you've selected, fill
in the blank spaces in the story.
Now you've created your own hilarious MAD LIB!

THE POOR SPOTTED AUK

PLURAL NOUN: _____

PLURAL NOUN: _____

ADJECTIVE: _____

ADJECTIVE: _____

AN ANIMAL: _____

PLURAL NOUN: _____

PLURAL NOUN: _____

NOUN: _____

ADJECTIVE: _____

ADJECTIVE: _____

THE POOR SPOTTED AUK

The auk is a bird which will soon be extinct because hunters keep

shooting them so they can sell their _____ to women
                                        PLURAL NOUN

who wear them on their_____. The Government should
                        PLURAL NOUN

establish _____ game preserves where auks can build
            ADJECTIVE

nests and lay eggs, and where they would be safe from their natural

enemies, the _____ otter and the underwater
                 ADJECTIVE

_____. Otters sneak up and eat the poor auk's
    AN ANIMAL

_____. Of course, a female auk can lay five thousand
  PLURAL NOUN

_____ a year and if they all hatched, in a short time we
  PLURAL NOUN

would all be up to our _____ in auks. Remember, a/an
                          NOUN

_____ auk is a/an _____ auk.
    ADJECTIVE   ADJECTIVE

MAD LIBS® is fun to play with friends, but you can also play it by yourself!
To begin with, DO NOT look at the story on the page below. Fill in the blanks
on this page with the words called for. Then, using the words you've selected, fill
in the blank spaces in the story.
Now you've created your own hilarious MAD LIB!

LINK TRAINER & FLYING

ADJECTIVE: _____

NOUN: _____

PLURAL NOUN: _____

NOUN: _____

PLURAL NOUN: _____

NOUN: _____

ADJECTIVE: _____

NOUN: _____

NOUN: _____

NOUN: _____

NOUN: _____

A COLOR: _____

NUMBER: _____

NUMBER: _____

LINK TRAINER & FLYING

A Link Trainer is a/an _____ airplane that never leaves the
ADJECTIVE

_____. It's used to teach beginning _____
NOUN   PLURAL NOUN

the principles of flying. It has a/an _____ and a full set
NOUN

of _____ just like a regular airplane. And it can imitate
PLURAL NOUN

any sort of aerial maneuver such as a loop the _____ or a/an
NOUN

_____ dive. And it is very safe. Nothing can happen to
ADJECTIVE

you unless, of course, you forget to fasten your safety _____.
NOUN

Then you might fall out on your _____.
NOUN

After a student passes the tests on the Link Trainer, he then gets into

a real plane and learns to taxi down the _____. And he
NOUN

learns to tell which way the _____ is blowing before he
NOUN

takes off into the "Wild _____ Yonder!" Then in no
A COLOR

time he learns to take off and is flying _____ miles per
NUMBER

hour at a height of _____ feet. When he does this, he is a
NUMBER

real pilot.

MAD LIBS® is fun to play with friends, but you can also play it by yourself!
To begin with, DO NOT look at the story on the page below. Fill in the blanks
on this page with the words called for. Then, using the words you've selected, fill
in the blank spaces in the story.
Now you've created your own hilarious MAD LIB!

FIRE FIGHTERS

ADJECTIVE: _____

NOUN: _____

NOUN: _____

PLURAL NOUN: _____

NUMBER: _____

NOUN: _____

NOUN: _____

ADJECTIVE: _____

A LIQUID: _____

PLURAL NOUN: _____

ADJECTIVE: _____

NOUN: _____

PLURAL NOUN: _____

NOUN: _____

FIRE FIGHTERS

When I was ten years old, my _____ ambition in life was
ADJECTIVE

to be a fire fighter—but here I am, nothing but a/an_____
ADJECTIVE

_____. If I were a fire fighter, I'd get to wear a huge, red
NOUN

_____. And I could ride on the fire engines that carry 80-foot
NOUN

_____and travel _____ miles an hour.
PLURAL NOUN   NUMBER

When fire engines blow their_____, all cars have to pull
PLURAL NOUN

over to the side of the_____. Fire departments have hook
NOUN

and_____ wagons as well as pump trucks which carry
ADJECTIVE

_____ hoses that pump _____into burning
ADJECTIVE   A LIQUID

_____. Fire fighters have to go into_____
PLURAL NOUN   ADJECTIVE

buildings and fight their way through smoke and_____to
NOUN

rescue any_____who may be trapped inside. We should
PLURAL NOUN

all be thankful that our fire fighters are on the job twenty-four hours

a/an_____.
NOUN

MAD LIBS® is fun to play with friends, but you can also play it by yourself!
To begin with, DO NOT look at the story on the page below. Fill in the blanks
on this page with the words called for. Then, using the words you've selected, fill
in the blank spaces in the story.
Now you've created your own hilarious MAD LIB!

SMOKING CIGARETTES

A DISEASE: _____

NOUN: _____

PART OF BODY: _____

ADJECTIVE: _____

NAME OF PERSON IN ROOM: _____

PLURAL NOUN: _____

PLURAL NOUN: _____

NASTY ADJECTIVE: _____

PLURAL NOUN: _____

EXCLAMATION: _____

PLURAL NOUN: _____

SMOKING CIGARETTES

Medical science has discovered that smoking cigarettes causes
_____. It is also bad for your _____ and
     A DISEASE   NOUN

causes pains in the _____.
                    PART OF BODY

When mice and dogs were exposed to _____ cigarette
                           ADJECTIVE

smoke, they developed _____'s disease. To-
               NAME OF PERSON IN ROOM

bacco companies have put charcoal _____ on the ends
                     PLURAL NOUN

of cigarettes, but they still spend millions of _____
                           PLURAL NOUN

advertising their _____ product.
         NASTY ADJECTIVE

If you smoke cigarettes, the tobacco will leave all kinds of tar and
_____ in your lungs. This will make you cough and say
   PLURAL NOUN

"_____!" Don't smoke cigarettes. Remember,
     EXCLAMATION

only _____ smoke.
    PLURAL NOUN